기초탄탄
GRAMMAR
2

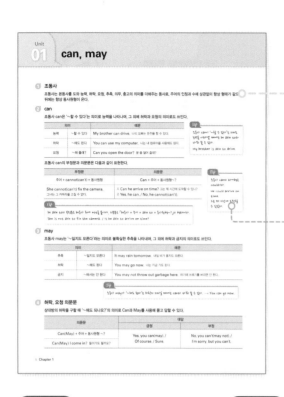

문법 개념 정리

문법의 핵심 포인트를 체계적으로 학습할 수 있도록
도표화하고 예문을 통해 쉽게 설명해 줍니다.

TIP

놓치기 쉬운, 그러나 꼭 기억해야 할 포인트를
콕 집어 알려 줍니다.

Grammar Start
개념 확인 문제

단원의 학습목표가 되는 문법 포인트를
콕 집어 그 원리를 확인하는 연습문제
입니다.

Grammar Practice
심화 학습 문제

틀린 부분 고쳐 쓰기, 문장 유형 바꿔
쓰기, 단어 배열하기, 영작하기 등 단원
의 핵심 문법 포인트를 문장 속에서 파
악할 수 있도록 심화된 학습을 합니다.

Upgrade Test
내신 테스트형 문제

학교 내신 유형의 문제로 단원 학습 내용을
통합 응용한 테스트형 문제입니다.

Word List

새로 나온 단어들의 우리말 뜻을 제공하여
문제풀이에 도움을 줍니다.

서술형 주관식

내신 서술형 주관식 문제로
실전감을 더욱 높일 수 있습니다.

Review Test

연계된 학습 흐름으로 구성된 두 개의 Chapter를 복습하는 문제로 다양한 유형을 다루어 줍니다.

Workbook

각 단원의 문법 포인트를 두 페이지의 문제풀이를 통해 확인학습 할 수 있습니다.

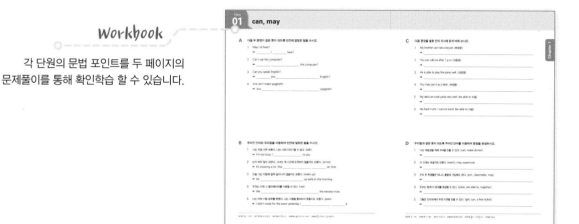

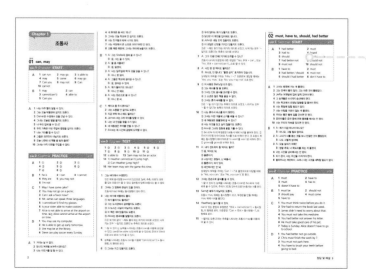

정답 및 해설

문장의 해석은 물론 내신형 문제의 문법 포인트를 친절하고 정확하게 해설해 줍니다.

Contents

기초 탄탄 2
GRAMMAR

Chapter
1

조동사

Unit 01 | can, may

① 조동사

조동사는 본동사를 도와 능력, 허락, 요청, 추측, 의무, 충고의 의미를 더해주는 동사로, 주어의 인칭과 수에 상관없이 항상 형태가 같으며, 뒤에는 항상 동사원형이 온다.

② can

조동사 can은 '~할 수 있다'는 의미로 능력을 나타내며, 그 외에 허락과 요청의 의미로도 쓰인다.

의미		예문
능력	~할 수 있다	My brother can drive. 나의 오빠는 운전을 할 수 있다.
허락	~해도 된다	You can use my computer. 너는 내 컴퓨터를 사용해도 된다.
요청	~해 줄래?	Can you open the door? 문 좀 열어 줄래?

> **Tip**
> 조동사 can이 '~할 수 있다'는 의미로 능력을 나타낼 때에는 be able to와 바꿔 쓸 수 있다.
> My brother is able to drive.

조동사 can의 부정문과 의문문은 다음과 같이 표현한다.

부정문	의문문
주어 + cannot(can't) + 동사원형	Can + 주어 + 동사원형 ~?
She cannot(can't) fix the camera. 그녀는 그 카메라를 고칠 수 없다.	A Can he arrive on time? 그는 제 시간에 도착할 수 있니? B Yes, he can. / No, he cannot(can't).

> **Tip**
> 조동사 can의 과거형은 could이다.
> He could arrive on time.
> 그는 제 시간에 도착할 수 있었다.

> **Tip**
> be able to의 부정문은 be동사 뒤에 not을 붙이며, 의문문은 『be동사 + 주어 + able to + 동사원형 ~?』의 형태이다.
> She is not able to fix the camera. / Is he able to arrive on time?

③ may

조동사 may는 '~일지도 모른다'라는 의미로 불확실한 추측을 나타내며, 그 외에 허락과 금지의 의미로도 쓰인다.

의미		예문
추측	~일지도 모른다	It may rain tomorrow. 내일 비가 올지도 모른다.
허락	~해도 된다	You may go now. 너는 지금 가도 된다.
금지	~해서는 안 된다	You may not throw out garbage here. 여기에 쓰레기를 버리면 안 된다.

> **Tip**
> 조동사 may가 '~해도 된다'는 허락의 의미일 때에는 can과 바꿔 쓸 수 있다. → You can go now.

④ 허락, 요청 의문문

상대방의 허락을 구할 때 '~해도 되나요?'의 의미로 Can과 May를 사용해 묻고 답할 수 있다.

의문문	대답	
	긍정	부정
Can(May) + 주어 + 동사원형 ~?	Yes, you can(may). / Of course. / Sure.	No, you can't(may not). / I'm sorry, but you can't.
Can(May) I come in? 들어가도 될까요?		

A 다음 괄호 안에서 알맞은 것을 고르시오.

1 I (can run / run can) very fast.

2 He (may goes / may go) to the museum today.

3 Daniel (is able to / can to) swim across the river.

4 She (may / may to) see the stars tonight.

5 Can you (come / comes) to my house?

6 My family (may go / go may) camping this weekend.

7 (Can you / May you) play the guitar?

8 They (may not / not may) be foreigners.

9 (Can / May) you lend me your books today?

10 She (be able to / cannot) buy a ticket yet.

fast 빨리
museum 박물관
across 건너서
go camping 캠핑을 가다
foreigner 외국인
lend 빌려주다
yet (부정문, 의문문에서) 아직

B 다음 우리말과 같은 뜻이 되도록 밑줄 친 부분을 바르게 고쳐 쓰시오.

1 곧 비가 올지도 모른다.

It <u>can</u> rain soon. ➡ _____

2 우리는 이 의자를 옮길 수 있다.

We <u>may</u> carry this chair. ➡ _____

3 Sam은 중국어를 말할 수 없다.

Sam <u>may not</u> speak Chinese. ➡ _____

4 너는 이 문제를 풀 수 있니?

Are you <u>going to</u> solve this problem? ➡ _____

5 창문 좀 열어줄래?

<u>May I</u> open the window? ➡ _____

carry 옮기다, 나르다
solve 풀다, 해결하다

A 다음 밑줄 친 조동사의 의미로 가장 적절한 것을 보기에서 고르시오.

| 보기 | ① 능력 | ② 허락, 요청 | ③ 추측 | ④ 금지 |

passport 여권
loudly 크게
theater 극장
because of ~ ~ 때문에
traffic jam 교통 체증

1 Spiders <u>cannot</u> fly. _____

2 <u>May</u> I see your passport? _____

3 I <u>can</u> ride a bicycle well. _____

4 <u>Can</u> I use your cellphone? _____

5 She <u>may</u> not go to school today. _____

6 You <u>can</u> go outside with your friends. _____

7 You <u>may not</u> talk loudly in the theater. _____

8 Because of the traffic jam, she <u>may</u> be late for the party. _____

B 다음 대화의 빈칸에 알맞은 말을 쓰시오.

turn off (불을) 끄다
left 왼쪽의

1 A Is he able to come to Stella's house?
   B Yes, _____ _____ .

2 A Can you turn off the light?
   B Yes, _____ _____ .

3 A Can you read two books in a week?
   B No, _____ _____ .

4 A Are they able to walk to their school?
   B Yes, _____ _____ .

5 A May I come in?
   B No, _____ _____ _____ .

6 A Are you able to write with your left hand?
   B No, _____ _____ .

C 틀린 부분을 찾아 바르게 고쳐 문장을 다시 쓰시오.

1 May I has some cake?

   ➡ _____

2 You not may go on a picnic.

   ➡ _____

3 Can I asking a favor now?

   ➡ _____

4 Mr. James cans speak three languages.

   ➡ _____

5 I can not find my glasses.

   ➡ _____

6 Are your sister able to make cookies?

   ➡ _____

7 Alice cannot able to arrive at the airport on time.

   ➡ _____

go on a picnic 소풍 가다
favor 부탁
arrive 도착하다
airport 공항

D 우리말과 같은 뜻이 되도록 주어진 단어를 바르게 배열하시오.

1 네가 내 컴퓨터를 사용해도 좋아. (use, may, you, computer, my)

   ➡ _____

2 그는 내일 일찍 일어날 수 있다. (is, get up, he, to, tomorrow, able, early)

   ➡ _____

3 그녀는 도서관에 있을지도 모른다. (at, may, the library, she, be)

   ➡ _____

4 Steve는 매주 일요일 축구를 할 수 있다. (soccer, Sunday, can, every, Steve, play)

   ➡ _____

get up 일어나다
early 일찍
library 도서관

1 빈칸에 들어갈 수 <u>없는</u> 것을 고르시오.

> He _____ swim in the sea.

① can   ② will   ③ is
④ may   ⑤ is able to

2 빈칸에 들어갈 알맞은 것을 고르시오.

> She may _____ interested in the movie.

① be   ② are   ③ is
④ was   ⑤ were

3 다음 밑줄 친 부분과 의미가 같은 것을 고르시오.

> You <u>may</u> stay here.

① <u>May</u> I come in?
② He <u>may</u> study in the library.
③ The news <u>may</u> not be true.
④ This book <u>may</u> be interesting.
⑤ Alice <u>may</u> speak Chinese well.

4 다음 우리말과 같은 뜻이 되도록 빈칸에 들어갈 알맞은 것을 고르시오.

> 우리는 그곳에서 무슨 옷이든 입어 볼 수 있다.
> = We _____ try on any clothes there.

① able to   ② be able to   ③ can
④ could   ⑤ cannot

5 다음 우리말을 영어로 바르게 옮긴 것을 고르시오.

> Tony는 그 질문에 답할 수 없다.

① Tony don't answer the question.
② Tony doesn't answers the question.
③ Tony not can answer the question.
④ Tony cannot answer the question.
⑤ Tony can't speaks answer the question.

6 밑줄 친 부분의 의미가 나머지와 <u>다른</u> 것을 고르시오.

① She <u>may</u> be sleeping.
② My mom <u>may</u> get angry.
③ You <u>may</u> try on this jacket.
④ John <u>may</u> not come tomorrow.
⑤ This fruit <u>may</u> have a sour taste.

[7-8] 빈칸에 들어갈 알맞은 말을 고르시오.

7
> A Can he get there in 10 minutes?
> B _____

① Yes, he is.   ② Yes, he will.
③ Yes, he could.   ④ No, he can.
⑤ No, he can't.

be interested in ~ ~에 관심이 있다 stay 머무르다 clothes 옷, 의복 answer 대답하다 question 질문 sour 신, 시큼한

8

> A May I take a picture?
>
> B _____ There's a sign that says,
>   "No Photographs."

① Yes, you may.   ② Yes, you could.

③ No, you don't.   ④ No, you may not.

⑤ No, you could not.

9 밑줄 친 부분의 쓰임이 나머지와 <u>다른</u> 것을 고르시오.

① That <u>cannot</u> be Betty.

② He <u>cannot</u> play rugby.

③ She <u>cannot</u> cook Indian food.

④ The boy <u>cannot</u> carry many books.

⑤ She <u>cannot</u> do her homework alone.

10 다음 중 어법상 올바른 문장을 고르시오.

① I'm able not to take a bus alone.

② Can she learn to ski this winter?

③ Are your sister able to go to the zoo?

④ You may not to want to believe this.

⑤ Ann can grows flowers in her garden.

11 다음 질문에 대한 답으로 알맞지 <u>않은</u> 것을 고르시오.

> A Can I have some sandwiches?
>
> B _____

① Yes, you can.

② Of course.

③ No, thanks. I'm full.

④ Sure. Here you are.

⑤ I'm sorry, but you can't.

12 다음 두 문장이 같은 뜻이 되도록 빈칸에 들어갈
알맞은 말을 쓰시오.

> She can write with her left hand.
>
> = She _____ _____ _____ write
>   with her left hand.

→ _____

13 어법상 어색한 부분을 찾아 바르게 고쳐 문장을
다시 쓰시오.

> Sam is not may be an actor.

→ _____

14 다음 문장을 부정문과 의문문으로 바꾸시오.

> Heather can jump high.

1) 부정문 _____

2) 의문문 _____

15 주어진 단어를 이용하여 다음 우리말을 영어로
쓰시오.

> 그녀의 팀은 이번에 그 경기에서 이길지도 모른다.
>
> (win the game, this time)

→ _____

_____

---

sign 표지판 photograph 사진 rugby 럭비 Indian 인도의 carry 나르다 do one's homework 숙제를 하다 believe 믿다 grow 기르다
high 높게 win a game 경기에서 이기다

must, have to, should, had better

1 must, have to

조동사 must는 '~해야 한다'라는 의미로 have to와 바꿔 쓸 수 있으며, '~임에 틀림 없다'라는 추측의 의미로도 쓴다.

조동사	의미	예문
must	의무 (~해야 한다)	You must submit your homework. 너는 숙제를 제출해야 한다.
	추측 (~임에 틀림 없다)	He must be honest. 그는 정직함에 틀림없다.
have to	의무 (~해야 한다)	You have to submit your homework. 너는 숙제를 제출해야 한다.

Tip

must의 과거형은 had to로 쓴다.
You had to submit your homework then.
너는 그때 숙제를 제출해야 했다.

Tip

의무를 묻는 의문문은 『Do/Does + 주어 + have to + 동사원형 ~?』의 형태로 쓴다.
Do I have to write a letter to Mr. Brown? 제가 Brown 씨께 편지를 써야 하나요?

조동사 must와 have의 부정문은 다음과 같이 쓴다.

조동사	부정형	의미	예문
must	must not	강한 금지 (~해서는 안 된다)	You must not run in the library. 너는 도서관에서 뛰어서는 안 된다.
have to	don't have to	불필요 (~할 필요가 없다)	We don't have to hurry. 우리는 서두를 필요가 없다.

Tip

don't have to는 don't need to로 바꿔 쓸 수 있다.
= we don't need to hurry.
과거형은 둘 다 don't를 didn't로 바꾼다.

2 should, had better

조동사 should는 '~해야 한다'라는 의미로 도덕적 의무나 충고를 나타내며, 조동사 had better는 '~하는 게 좋겠다'라는 강한 충고나 권유를 나타낸다.

조동사	의미	예문
should	의무 (~해야 한다)	We should respect your parents. 우리는 부모님을 공경해야 한다.
had better	강한 충고, 권유 (~하는 게 좋겠다)	You had better go to bed now. 너는 지금 잠을 자는 게 낫겠다.

Tip

had better는 'd better로 줄여서 쓸 수 있다.

조동사 should와 had better의 부정문은 다음과 같이 쓴다.

조동사	부정형	의미	예문
should	should not = shouldn't	강한 금지 (~해서는 안 된다)	You shouldn't eat too much chocolate. 너는 너무 많은 초콜릿을 먹으면 안 된다.
had better	had better not = 'd better not	강한 충고 (~하지 않는 게 좋겠다)	You had better not eat a lot of fast food. 너는 패스트푸드를 많이 먹지 않는 게 좋겠다.

Tip

had better의 부정형은 had not better로 쓰지 않고 had better not으로 쓰는 것에 유의한다.

A 다음 괄호 안에서 알맞은 것을 고르시오.

1 She (has better / had better) see a doctor.

2 He doesn't look good. He (must / have to) be sick.

3 Jeff (must / had to) go home early last night.

4 The passengers should (board / to board) the ship by 4.

5 You (should / should to) listen to the teachers at school.

6 You (need not to / don't have to) work during the holiday.

7 You (had not better / had better not) skip breakfast.

8 We (should not / don't need to) cross the street at a red light.

9 Drivers (must not / don't have to) talk on the phone while driving.

10 You (don't should / should not) forget our appointment.

passenger 승객
board 승선하다, 승차하다
holiday 휴일
cross 건너다
skip 거르다
breakfast 아침
while ~하는 동안
driving 운전
appointment 약속

B 다음 문장에서 알맞은 말을 보기에서 골라 쓰시오. (단, 한 번씩만 쓸 것)

| 보기 | must   have to   must not   don't have to   should   had better |

1 A Do I _____ leave now?

   B No, you don't need to.

2 A She _____ be very friendly to help you.

   B I think so, too.

3 A How is the weather today?

   B It's very cold. You _____ wear a scarf.

4 You _____ waste your time.

5 It's raining. You _____ take your umbrella.

6 The blouse is clean. So you _____ wash it.

leave 떠나다
friendly 친절한, 상냥한
wear 입다
scarf 목도리, 스카프
waste 낭비하다
take 가지고 가다
blouse 블라우스

Grammar **PRACTICE**

A 다음 두 문장이 같은 의미가 되도록 빈칸에 알맞은 말을 쓰시오.

1 I am sure that he is very rich.

= He _____ be very rich.

2 You must do your homework now.

= You _____ _____ do your homework now.

3 It is necessary that you should go there.

= You _____ go there.

4 Andy must follow the school rules.

= Andy _____ _____ follow the school rules.

5 She doesn't need to attend the meeting.

= She _____ _____ _____ attend the meeting.

necessary 필요한
It is necessary
~할 필요가 있다
follow 따르다
attend 참석하다

B 주어진 단어와 우리말을 이용하여 빈칸에 알맞은 말을 쓰시오.

1 이 우유는 맛이 이상하다. 그것은 상했음이 틀림없다. (must)

➡ This milk tastes strange. It _____ _____ go bad.

2 우리는 약속을 어기면 안 된다. 그것은 신뢰의 문제이다. (should)

➡ We _____ _____ break our word. It is a question of trust.

3 날씨가 나날이 추워지고 있다. 너는 네 건강에 주의를 기울여야 한다. (should, pay)

➡ It's getting colder day by day. You _____ _____ attention to your health.

4 3시에 회의가 있다. 나는 2시 전까지 사무실에 들어와야 한다. (must, come)

➡ The meeting is at 3 o'clock. I _____ _____ to my office before 2.

5 그녀의 상태가 점점 나빠지고 있다. 의사들은 그녀를 수술해야 한다. (have to)

➡ Her condition is getting worse. The doctors _____ _____ operate on her.

taste 맛이 나다
strange 이상한
break one's word
약속을 어기다
trust 신뢰
pay attention to ~
~에 주목하다
meeting 회의
operate 수술하다

C 틀린 부분을 찾아 바르게 고쳐 문장을 다시 쓰시오.

1 You must to think twice before you do it.

   ➡ _____

2 She has to return the book last week.

   ➡ _____

3 James didn't to need worry about that.

   ➡ _____

4 You don't must take this medicine.

   ➡ _____

5 You have better not answer his letter.

   ➡ _____

6 He musts take good care of his pet.

   ➡ _____

7 Today is Sunday. Alice don't have to go to school.

   ➡ _____

twice 두 번
return 돌아오다
worry 걱정하다
medicine 약
letter 편지
take care of ~ ~을 돌보다

D 우리말과 같은 뜻이 되도록 주어진 단어를 바르게 배열하시오.

1 너는 밖에 나가지 않는 게 좋겠다. (go, had, you, better, outside, not)

   ➡ _____

2 Chris는 그 일을 7시까지 끝내야 한다. (finish, by 7, the work, must, Chris)

   ➡ _____

3 당신은 여기에 주차하면 안 됩니다. (here, you, not, park, must)

   ➡ _____

4 너는 자기 전에 이를 닦아야 한다.
  (before, to, brush, you, have, going to bed, your teeth)

   ➡ _____

outside 바깥, 밖
park 주차하다

1 빈칸에 들어갈 알맞은 것을 고르시오.

> Alice is working without taking a break these days. She _____ be very tired.

① should ② cannot ③ must
④ need to ⑤ had better

2 밑줄 친 부분과 바꿔 쓸 수 있는 것을 고르시오.

> You don't have to write an answer in English.

① may not ② should not
③ must not ④ don't need to
⑤ had better not

3 다음 우리말과 같은 뜻이 되도록 빈칸에 알맞은 것을 고르시오.

> 너는 매일 운동을 해야 한다.
> = You _____ exercise every day.

① do ② should do
③ shouldn't do ④ must not do
⑤ must do to

4 빈칸에 들어갈 알맞은 것을 고르시오.

> You must come back today.
> = You _____ come back today.

① have to ② may
③ don't have to ④ could
⑤ should not to

5 다음 우리말을 영어로 바르게 옮긴 것을 고르시오.

> 너는 그곳에 혼자 가지 않는 게 좋겠다.

① You had not better go there alone.
② You had better not go there alone.
③ You had better not to go there alone.
④ You don't have better go there alone.
⑤ You didn't have better go there alone.

6 다음 문장을 의문문으로 바르게 바꾼 것을 고르시오.

> Sarah has to water the flowers.

① Do Sarah have to water the flowers?
② Do Sarah has to water the flowers?
③ Does Sarah have to water the flowers?
④ Does Sarah has to water the flowers?
⑤ Does have Sarah to water the flowers?

7 다음 중 우리말을 영어로 잘못 옮긴 것을 고르시오.

① 나는 내 친구를 기다려야 해.
　→ I have to wait for my friend.
② 그들은 지금 시청에 가야 해.
　→ They must go to city hall.
③ 너는 초콜릿을 먹어서는 안 돼.
　→ You must not eat chocolate.
④ 우리는 매일 교실을 청소해야 해.
　→ We must clean our classroom every day.
⑤ 그는 지금 떠나서는 안 돼.
　→ He doesn't have to leave now.

---

tired 피곤한 do exercise 운동을 하다 alone 혼자 water 물을 주다 wait for ~ ~를 기다리다 city hall 시청 leave 떠나다

8 빈칸에 must가 들어갈 수 <u>없는</u> 것을 고르시오.

① I _____ get some sleep.

② We _____ bring our books.

③ You _____ not eat fast food.

④ She _____ practice the flute last week.

⑤ He _____ be happy to meet his old friend.

9 다음 중 두 문장의 의미가 <u>다른</u> 것을 고르시오.

① I should take care of my brother.

= I have to take care of my brother.

② I have to check out a book about science.

= I should check out a book about science.

③ They should not wear their shoes here.

= They must not wear their shoes here.

④ You should not run in the restaurant.

= You don't have to run in the restaurant.

⑤ We must turn off our cellphones in class.

= We have to turn off our cellphones in class.

10 밑줄 친 부분의 의미가 나머지와 <u>다른</u> 것을 고르시오.

① You <u>must</u> listen to the teachers.

② The teacher <u>must</u> be upset with us.

③ <u>Must</u> I finish this project by noon?

④ You <u>must</u> tell the truth to everyone.

⑤ The students <u>must</u> put the books in the right place.

11 밑줄 친 부분의 쓰임이 <u>잘못된</u> 것을 고르시오.

① You <u>must not</u> take a picture here.

② You <u>don't have to</u> go to the bank.

③ You <u>had not better</u> lose your tickets.

④ Students <u>should not</u> move around during the contest.

⑤ You <u>should not enter</u> this building without permission.

12 다음 대화를 읽고, 주어진 단어를 바르게 배열하여 빈칸에 알맞은 말을 쓰시오.

> A Let's watch the new movie together.
>
> B I'm sorry. I _____ .
>
> (my mom, to, help, have)

→ _____

13 어법상 <u>어색한</u> 부분을 찾아 바르게 고쳐 문장을 다시 쓰시오.

> Daniel has to buy new glasses yesterday.

→ _____

14 다음 문장을 부정문과 의문문으로 바꿔 쓰시오.

> They should go to school early.

1) 부정문 _____

2) 의문문 _____

15 주어진 단어를 바르게 배열하여 다음 우리말을 영어로 쓰시오.

> 너는 매일 아침과 저녁에 이를 닦는 게 좋겠다.
>
> (better, every, your teeth, had, night, you, brush, and, morning)

→ _____

---

bring 가져오다 practice 연습하다 check out (도서관 등에서) 대출받다 upset 속상한, 불편한 project 프로젝트, 계획, 과제 noon 정오, 낮 12시
truth 진실 take a picture 사진을 찍다 permission 허락 brush one's teeth 이를 닦다

Chapter
2

There & It

There is/are

1 긍정문

There is/are 구문은 '~가 있다'라는 의미이다. There is 다음에는 단수명사가 오고, There are 다음에는 복수명사가 온다. 이 구문은 보통 장소를 나타내는 표현과 함께 쓴다.

There is	There are
There is + 단수명사	There are + 복수명사
There is a cat on the chair. 의자 위에 고양이 한 마리가 있다.	There are three dogs on the playground. 놀이터에 강아지 세 마리가 있다.

Tip

셀 수 없는 명사는 항상 단수 취급하므로, 셀 수 없는 명사 앞에는 There is가 온다.
There are some water in the cup. (X) → There is some water in the cup. (O) 그 컵에 약간의 물이 있다.

Tip

There is/are 구문의 과거형은 There was/were로 쓴다.
There was a pond in my town. 우리 동네에는 호수가 있었다.
There were some students in the classroom. 교실에는 몇몇의 학생이 있었다.

Tip

여기에서 there은 유도부사로, 어떤 대상을 유도하기 위해 문장의 맨 앞에 쓰는 부사이다.
이때, there은 '거기에, 그곳에'라고 해석하지 않는다.

2 부정문

There is/are 구문의 부정문은 be동사 뒤에 not을 쓰고 '~가 없다'라고 해석한다.

There is	There are
There is + not + 단수명사	There are + not + 복수명사
There isn't an eraser in my pencil case. 내 필통 안에 지우개가 전혀 없다.	There aren't any flowers in the vase. 꽃병 안에는 꽃이 전혀 없다.

3 의문문

There is/are 구문의 의문문은 be동사와 There의 위치를 바꾸고, 문장 끝에 물음표를 붙인다. '~이 있니?'라고 해석한다.

There is	There are
Is there + 단수명사 ~?	Are there + 복수명사 ~?
A Is there a post office near here? 이 근처에 우체국이 있니? B Yes, there is. 응, 있어. / No, there isn't. 아니, 없어.	A Are there people on the street? 거리에 사람들이 있니? B Yes, there are. 응, 있어. / No, there aren't. 아니, 없어.

Tip

'얼마나 많은 ~가 있니?'라는 질문은 How many/much ~ is/are there?의 형태이다. 대답은 There is/are 구문으로 한다.
A How many people are there on the bus? 버스 안에 사람이 몇 명이 있니?
B There are five people on the bus. 그 버스에는 다섯 명이 있어.
A How much money is there in the piggy bank? 그 돼지저금통에 얼마가 있니?
B There is fifty dollars in the piggy bank. 그 돼지저금통에는 50달러가 있어.

Grammar START

A 다음 괄호 안에서 알맞은 것을 고르시오.

1   There (is / are) a bed in my room.

2   There (is / are) a restaurant on the corner.

3   There (is / are) two pictures on the wall.

4   There (is / are) many children on the street.

5   There (is / are) very much money in her wallet.

6   There (is / are) many snacks in my bag.

7   There (is / are) so many flowers in the garden.

8   There (is not / are not) a computer on the desk.

9   There (isn't / aren't) any books on the shelf.

10   There (isn't / aren't) enough water in the bottle.

corner 모서리, 모퉁이
wall 벽
wallet 지갑
snack 간식
garden 정원
any (부정문, 의문문에서)
전혀, 조금도
shelf 선반, 책꽂이
enough 충분한
bottle 병

B 다음 문장의 빈칸에 들어갈 알맞은 말을 쓰시오.

1   A Is there a map on the wall?

    B Yes, _____ _____ .

2   A Are there many apples in the basket?

    B No, _____ _____ .

3   A Are there many benches in the park?

    B Yes, _____ _____ .

4   A Are there lots of eggs on the table?

    B No, _____ _____ .

5   A How many balls are there in the box?

    B _____ _____ twenty balls in the box.

map 지도
bench 벤치
basket 바구니

Grammar **PRACTICE**

A 주어진 우리말을 이용하여 빈칸에 알맞은 말을 쓰시오.

1 거실에 소파 하나가 있다.

➡ _____ _____ a sofa in the living room.

2 땅 위에는 많은 눈이 있다.

➡ _____ _____ lots of snow on the ground.

3 동물원에 많은 코끼리들이 있다.

➡ _____ _____ many elephants in the zoo.

4 이 마을에는 다리 하나가 있다.

➡ _____ _____ a bridge in this town.

5 도로에 많은 표지판들이 있다.

➡ _____ _____ a lot of signs on the road.

6 나무 꼭대기에 새가 있니?

➡ _____ _____ a bird at the top of the tree?

7 네 필통엔 얼마나 많은 연필이 있니?

➡ _____ _____ pencils _____ there in your pencil case?

ground 땅, 지면
elephant 코끼리
bridge 다리
sign 표지판
road 도로
top 맨 위, 꼭대기
bird 새
pencil case 필통

B 밑줄 친 부분을 바르게 고쳐 쓰시오.

1 There <u>is</u> a lot of people in the picture. ➡ _____

2 There <u>isn't</u> three boxes on the shelf. ➡ _____

3 <u>Are</u> there a slice of toast on the table? ➡ _____

4 <u>Is</u> there two interesting stories in this book? ➡ _____

5 There <u>aren't</u> any orange juice in the refrigerator. ➡ _____

6 How <u>many</u> money is there in your pocket? ➡ _____

toast 토스트, 구운 빵
a slice of ~ ~의 한 조각
interesting 재미있는
refrigerator 냉장고
pocket 주머니

C 다음 문장을 부정문과 의문문으로 바꿔 쓰시오.

1 There is a pillow on the bed.

   ➡ _____

   ➡ _____

2 There are five people in her family.

   ➡ _____

   ➡ _____

3 There are many dishes in the kitchen.

   ➡ _____

   ➡ _____

4 There are four people in the office.

   ➡ _____

   ➡ _____

5 There is a gym in his school.

   ➡ _____

   ➡ _____

pillow 베개
dish 접시
office 사무실
gym 체육관

D 주어진 단어와 There is/are 구문을 이용하여 다음 우리말을 영어로 쓰시오.

1 하늘에 많은 별들이 있다. (many, stars, in the sky)

   ➡ _____

2 우리 집 앞에 오래된 나무 한 그루가 있다. (old tree, in front of)

   ➡ _____

3 우리 집 근처에 제과점이 하나 있다. (bakery, near)

   ➡ _____

4 인천에는 국제공항이 하나 있다. (international airport, in Incheon)

   ➡ _____

in front of ~ ~의 앞에
bakery 제과점
near 가까이에
international airport
국제공항

1 빈칸에 들어갈 알맞은 것을 고르시오.

> There _____ a lot of water in the water tank.

① be   ② is   ③ are
④ were   ⑤ being

2 빈칸에 들어갈 수 <u>없는</u> 것을 고르시오.

> There are _____.

① shoes in the store
② ducks on the pond
③ flowers in the vase
④ ten horses on the farm
⑤ some paper on the desk

3 빈칸에 들어갈 말이 바르게 짝지어진 것을 고르시오.

> • There _____ a ballpark in my town.
> • _____ there any special places in your city?

① is - Is   ② are - Is   ③ is - Are
④ are - Are   ⑤ be – Is

4 다음 우리말을 영어로 바르게 옮긴 것을 고르시오.

> 동물원에는 동물들이 많이 있다.

① There is lots of animals in the zoo.
② There was lots of animals in the zoo.
③ There be lots of animals in the zoo.
④ There are lots of animals in the zoo.
⑤ There has lots of animals in the zoo.

5 다음 질문에 대한 대답으로 알맞은 것을 고르시오.

> Is there a movie theater around here?

① Yes, there is.
② No, there is.
③ Yes, there are.
④ Yes, there was.
⑤ No, there aren't.

6 다음 두 문장이 같은 뜻이 되도록 빈칸에 알맞은 것을 고르시오.

> My school has a computer room and a swimming pool.
>
> = _____ a computer room and a swimming pool at my school.

① It is   ② There are   ③ There has
④ There is   ⑤ There have

7 밑줄 친 부분의 쓰임이 나머지와 <u>다른</u> 것을 고르시오.

① Is <u>there</u> any extra food?
② <u>There</u> are toys in the box.
③ The girl over <u>there</u> is my sister.
④ Is <u>there</u> a pencil in your pencil case?
⑤ <u>There</u> are a lot of people on the bus.

---

water tank 물탱크, 수조   pond 연못   farm 농장   ballpark 야구장   extra 여분의

8 다음 중 빈칸에 들어갈 말이 나머지와 <u>다른</u> 것을 고르시오.

① There _____ a lot of snow in January.
② There _____ a cup of tea on the table.
③ There _____ some candy on the sofa.
④ There _____ two soccer balls in the field.
⑤ There _____ some money in her wallet.

9 다음 문장과 바꿔 쓸 수 있는 것을 고르시오.

> The bookstore has many kinds of books.

① There is many kinds of books in the bookstore.
② There are many kinds of books in the bookstore.
③ There be many kinds of books in the bookstore.
④ There has many kinds of books in the bookstore.
⑤ There have many kinds of books in the bookstore.

10 다음 중 어법상 <u>어색한</u> 문장을 고르시오.

① There is an umbrella on the desk.
② There is a woman at the bus stop.
③ There aren't a table in the kitchen.
④ Is there a house on top of the hill?
⑤ There are 24 hours in a day.

11 어법상 <u>틀린</u> 문장의 개수를 고르시오.

- There isn't anyone in the house.
- There are much smoke in the kitchen.
- There are many kites in the sky.
- Are there lots of people at the party?
- There is some orange juice in the cup.

① 1개   ② 2개   ③ 3개
④ 4개   ⑤ 5개

12 다음 두 문장이 같은 뜻이 되도록 빈칸에 들어갈 알맞은 말을 쓰시오.

> My house has two TVs.
>
> = _____ _____ _____ _____
> in my house.

→ _____

13 다음 문장을 부정문과 의문문으로 바꿔 쓰시오.

> There is an animal clinic nearby.

1) 부정문 _____
2) 의문문 _____

14 다음 대화의 빈칸에 알맞은 말을 쓰시오.

> A _____ _____ many cars in
> the parking lot?
> 주차장에 차가 많이 있나요?
>
> B _____, _____ _____.
> 아니요, 없습니다.

15 주어진 단어를 이용하여 다음 우리말을 영어로 쓰시오.

> 우리 학교 축제에는 특별한 이벤트가 있다.
>
> (a special event, at my school festival)

→ _____

_____

field 경기장 bookstore 서점 kind 종류 smoke 연기 kite 연 animal clinic 동물 병원 nearby 근처에 parking lot 주차장
school festival 학교 축제

Unit 02 | 비인칭 주어 it

1 비인칭 주어 it

시간, 날짜, 요일, 날씨, 거리, 계절, 명암 등을 나타낼 때 it을 주어로 써서 표현하는데, 이때 it을 비인칭 주어라고 한다.

비인칭 주어 it	예문
시간	It is 3 o'clock. 3시이다.
날짜	It is May 27. 5월 27일이다.
요일	It is Wednesday. 수요일이다.
날씨	It is cold and windy. 바람이 불고 춥다.
거리	It is 4 kilometers from here. 여기에서 4킬로미터이다.
계절	It is spring now. 지금은 봄이다.
명암	It is very bright outside. 바깥은 매우 밝다.

> **TIP**
> 비인칭 주어 it은 '그것'이라고 해석하지 않는다. '그것'이라고 해석하는 대명사 it과 구별해서 사용해야 한다.

2 비인칭 주어 it 의문문

비인칭 주어 it의 쓰임에 따라 사용하는 의문문은 다음과 같다.

비인칭 주어 it	예문
시간	A What time is it? 몇시니? B It is 12:30. 12시 30분이야.
날짜	A What date is it today? 오늘은 며칠이니? B It is October 21. 10월 21일이야.
요일	A What day is it today? 오늘은 무슨 요일이니? B It is Sunday. 일요일이야.
날씨	A How is the weather? / What is the weather like? 날씨가 어떠니? B It is sunny. 날씨가 맑아.
거리	A How far is it from here to school? 여기에서 학교까지 거리가 얼마나 되니? B It is 3 kilometers from here. 여기에서 3킬로미터야.
계절	A What season is it? 무슨 계절이니? B It is summer now. 지금은 여름이야.

3 it의 다양한 쓰임

대명사 it, 비인칭 주어 it, 그리고 가주어 it은 다음과 같이 구분된다.

it의 쓰임	예문
대명사	It is my pencil. 그것은 나의 연필이다.
비인칭 주어	It is 5 o'clock. 5시이다.
가주어	It is important to finish the work in time. 제시간에 그 일을 끝내는 것이 중요하다.

> **TIP**
> 주어의 길이가 길 때 문장의 안정감을 주기 위해 긴 주어를 문장의 뒤로 보내고 주어 자리에 가주어 it을 쓴다. 비인칭 주어 it과 가주어 it은 '그것'이라고 해석하지 않는다.

Grammar START

A 다음 문장에서 밑줄 친 비인칭 주어 it의 쓰임을 보기에서 골라 쓰시오.

보기	① 시간	② 날짜	③ 거리	④ 날씨	⑤ 요일

1 It is Friday. _____

2 It is sunny and warm. _____

3 It is far from Toronto to Vancouver. _____

4 It is 9 in the morning. _____

5 It is rainy outside. _____

6 It is August 7 today. _____

7 It is about 10 kilometers. _____

8 It is cloudy in London. _____

Friday 금요일
warm 따뜻한
Toronto 토론토
Vancouver 밴쿠버
August 8월
London 런던

B 다음 문장에서 밑줄 친 it의 쓰임 중 알맞은 것을 보기에서 골라 쓰시오.

보기	① 비인칭 주어	② 대명사	③ 가주어

1 Hurry up! It's already 2 o'clock. _____

2 There is a red umbrella. It's hers. _____

3 Why are you in a hurry? It's only 7 o'clock. _____

4 I bought a new dress. It's too tight for me. _____

5 It takes about thirty minutes by bus. _____

6 It's Sunday. But I woke up early. _____

7 It is dangerous to ride a bike at night. _____

8 A How is the weather in Daegu? B It's very hot. _____

already 이미, 벌써
tight 꽉 조이는, 딱 붙는
take (시간이) 걸리다
wake up (잠에서) 깨다, 일어나다
dangerous 위험한
ride 타다
bike 자전거

Grammar **PRACTICE**

A 보기에서 알맞은 말을 골라, 비인칭 주어 it을 이용하여 대화를 완성하시오. (축약형으로)

보기	Thursday	autumn in New York	snowing outside
	April 10	2 kilometers away	twelve o'clock

autumn 가을
outside 바깥
April 4월
Thursday 목요일
weather 날씨
season 계절

1 A What time is it?

   B _____

2 A What date is it today?

   B _____

3 A How is the weather?

   B _____

4 A How far is it?

   B _____

5 A What day is it today?

   B _____

6 A What season is it there?

   B _____

B 주어진 단어와 우리말을 이용하여 빈칸에 알맞은 말을 쓰시오. (축약형으로)

1 지금 호주는 겨울이다. (winter)

   ➡ _____ _____ in Australia now.

2 여름에는 비가 많이 온다. (rain)

   ➡ _____ _____ a lot in summer.

3 오늘은 학교 첫날이다. (first day)

   ➡ _____ the _____ _____ of school today.

4 우리 집에서 은행까지는 5마일의 거리이다. (miles)

   ➡ _____ 5 _____ from my house to the bank.

Australia 오스트레일리아, 호주
rain 비가 오다
a lot 많이
bank 은행

C 괄호 안의 단어를 이용하여 대화를 완성하시오. (축약형으로)

1 A What time is it now? (8:10)

   B _____

2 A What's the weather like? (fine and nice)

   B _____

3 A How far is it from here to the theater? (about 7 kilometers)

   B _____

4 A What date is it? (June 16)

   B _____

5 A What day is it today? (Monday)

   B _____

6 A What season is it? (spring)

   B _____

fine 맑은, 좋은
nice 좋은, 멋진
June 6월
Monday 월요일
spring 봄

D 우리말과 같은 뜻이 되도록 주어진 단어를 바르게 배열하시오.

1 지금은 초겨울이다. (winter, early, now, is, it)

   ➡ _____

2 밖은 약간 춥다. (is, outside, cold, it, little)

   ➡ _____

3 지금 시간은 11시 15분이다. (is, fifteen, it, eleven)

   ➡ _____

4 아직 밖이 환하다. (bright, still, is, outside, it)

   ➡ _____

5 일을 끝내는 데 얼마나 걸리니? (does, the work, to finish, how, it, long, take)

   ➡ _____

early winter 초겨울
still 여전히, 아직도
bright 밝은

[1-2] 빈칸에 들어갈 알맞은 것을 고르시오.

1

> _____ is April 16 today.

① It   ② Its   ③ This
④ That   ⑤ These

2

> A   Is it raining outside now?
>
> B   _____ It cleared up.

① Yes, it is.   ② Yes, it isn't.
③ No, it isn't.   ④ No, it doesn't.
⑤ Not, it is.

3 밑줄 친 it의 쓰임이 보기와 <u>다른</u> 것을 고르시오.

> It is 4 miles.

① How far is <u>it</u>?
② <u>It</u> is 40 dollars.
③ <u>It</u> is dark outside.
④ <u>It</u> is foggy and windy.
⑤ <u>It</u> is 7 in the morning.

4 빈칸에 들어갈 알맞은 것을 고르시오.

> What's the weather _____ in London?

① of   ② from   ③ about
④ around   ⑤ like

5 빈칸에 들어갈 알맞은 말을 고르시오.

> A   _____
>
> B   It is so cold.

① What day is it?
② What date is it?
③ What's the weather?
④ How is the weather?
⑤ What's time is it?

6 밑줄 친 it의 쓰임이 보기와 <u>다른</u> 것을 고르시오.

> <u>It</u> is Tuesday today.

① <u>It</u>'s 9:50.
② <u>It</u> will rain soon.
③ <u>It</u> is warm today.
④ <u>It</u> looks so cute.
⑤ What time is <u>it</u> now?

7 다음 중 it의 쓰임이 나머지와 <u>다른</u> 것을 고르시오.
① <u>It</u> is 5 o'clock.
② <u>It</u> was my mistake.
③ <u>It</u> is 8 in the evening.
④ Is <u>it</u> still snowing outside?
⑤ <u>It</u> takes 2 hours by train.

---

clear up (날씨가) 개다   dark 어두운   foggy 안개가 낀   windy 바람이 부는   cute 귀여운   mistake 실수

8 빈칸에 들어갈 말이 나머지와 <u>다른</u> 것을 고르시오.

① _____ is spring.
② _____ is warm and dry.
③ Isn't _____ too hot here?
④ _____ is six fifteen.
⑤ _____ is a dog in the park.

9 다음 중 it의 쓰임이 나머지와 <u>다른</u> 것을 고르시오.

① What time is <u>it</u>?
② <u>It</u> is easy to read the book.
③ <u>It's</u> summer, but it's not hot.
④ <u>It</u> was really stormy last night.
⑤ How long does <u>it</u> take to get there?

10 다음 중 it이 비인칭 주어로 쓰인 문장으로 짝지어진 것을 고르시오.

(A) Isn't <u>it</u> funny?
(B) <u>It's</u> nice to see you here.
(C) Is <u>it</u> his favorite subject?
(D) How far is <u>it</u> from here to your school?
(E) <u>It</u> is going to be sunny in the afternoon.

① (A), (B)   ② (A), (C)
③ (B), (D), (E)   ④ (D), (E)
⑤ (D)

11 다음 중 어법상 올바른 문장을 고르시오.

① That is winter.
② This is Saturday.
③ It will be cool.
④ Its doesn't bright at all.
⑤ That's already getting dark.

12 다음 두 문장이 같은 뜻이 되도록 빈칸에 알맞은 말을 쓰시오.

> We have a lot of rain in the rainy season.
> = _____ _____ rainy during the rainy season.

13 어법상 <u>어색한</u> 부분을 찾아 바르게 고쳐 쓰시오.

> That will soon be Chuseok.

_____ → _____

14 빈칸에 공통으로 들어갈 말을 쓰시오. (축약형으로)

> A What time is it now?
> B _____ 4:30.
> A What's the weather like today?
> B _____ snowy.

15 주어진 단어를 바르게 배열하여 다음 우리말을 영어로 쓰시오.

> L.A까지 가는 데 비행기로 14시간 정도 걸린다.
> (to New York, it, by airplane, 14 hours, takes, about)

→ _____
_____

dry 건조한   easy 쉬운   summer 여름   favorite 가장 좋아하는   subject 과목   Saturday 토요일   not at all 결코 ~하지 않는   rainy season 장마철
rainy 비가 많이 오는   during ~ ~동안에

1 빈칸에 들어갈 수 <u>없는</u> 것을 고르시오.

> You should _____.

① feed your dog
② get there by 4 p.m.
③ bring your ID card
④ wear your seatbelt
⑤ does exercise regularly

2 다음 문장을 부정문으로 만들 때, not이 들어갈 위치를 고르시오.

> You ① had ② better ③ make ④ any noise ⑤ in class.

[3-4] 밑줄 친 부분의 쓰임이 나머지와 <u>다른</u> 것을 고르시오.

3 ① <u>Can</u> you play the guitar?
② My mom <u>can</u> cook Indian food.
③ <u>Can</u> you tell me the time?
④ You <u>can</u> see a rainbow in the sky.
⑤ The bird <u>can</u> imitate human voices.

4 ① <u>It's</u> almost 5 p.m.
② <u>It</u> is September 3.
③ <u>It</u> is not Thursday.
④ <u>It's</u> my favorite color.
⑤ <u>It's</u> heavily raining outside.

5 다음 두 문장이 같은 뜻이 되도록 빈칸에 들어갈 알맞은 말을 쓰시오.

> You must turn off your cellphone during the movie.
>
> = You _____ _____ turn off your cellphone during the movie.

6 다음 우리말을 영어로 바르게 옮긴 것을 고르시오.

> 그녀는 교실에 없을지도 모른다.

① She may is not in the classroom.
② She may not is in the classroom.
③ She may not be in the classroom.
④ She may be not in the classroom.
⑤ She may be in the classroom.

7 빈칸에 들어갈 수 <u>없는</u> 것을 고르시오.

> There are _____ in the room.

① Jina   ② some students
③ many people   ④ soccer balls
⑤ a desk and a chair

8 빈칸에 들어갈 알맞은 것을 고르시오.

> She can hold her breath in the water for 30 seconds.
>
> = She _____ hold her breath in the water for 30 seconds.

① ables to   ② is able to   ③ are able to
④ has to   ⑤ must

9 빈칸에 들어갈 말이 바르게 짝지어진 것을 고르시오.

> A Is _____ a drugstore around here?
>
> B No, there _____ . You have to go two blocks.

① it - isn't 　　② it - cannot
③ there - hasn't 　　④ there - aren't
⑤ there - isn't

10 밑줄 친 부분이 어법상 올바른 것을 고르시오.

① There <u>are</u> only one bird in a cage.
② There <u>is</u> lots of water in the ocean.
③ There <u>is</u> many problems in the field.
④ There <u>are</u> some bread on the table.
⑤ There <u>is</u> a lot of students in the class.

11 주어진 단어를 이용하여 다음 우리말을 영어로 쓰시오.

> 너는 그 실수를 반복하면 안 된다.
>
> (must, repeat)

➡ You _____ the mistake.

12 다음 중 어법상 어색한 문장을 고르시오.

① Should I fill out this form?
② He has to pack his luggage.
③ I must be lock the front door.
④ I should practice the piano for 3 hours.
⑤ I am able to visit them in 2 weeks.

13 다음 짝지어진 두 문장의 의미가 <u>다른</u> 것을 고르시오.

① The bed must be comfortable.
　= The bed has to be comfortable.
② Will you turn down the radio?
　= Can you turn down the radio?
③ I couldn't go jogging yesterday.
　= I wasn't able to go jogging yesterday.
④ We don't have to take out the garbage.
　= We don't need to take out the garbage.
⑤ We should buy something for the party.
　= We had better buy something for the party.

[14-15] 다음 B의 스케줄 표와 대화를 읽고, 빈칸에 알맞은 말을 한 문장으로 쓰시오.

Wednesday	Thursday	Friday
5:00 p.m.	4:00 p.m.	10:00 a.m.
see a play	play basketball	go to speech class

> A Did you see a play yesterday?
>
> B Yes, I did. It was fun.

14

> A What time is it?
>
> B _____ I have to play basketball now.

15

> A What should you do on Friday?
>
> B _____

Chapter
3

형용사

형용사의 역할과 쓰임

1 형용사

형용사는 사람이나 사물의 생김새, 상태, 성질 등을 나타내는 말로, 명사를 꾸며주거나 주어를 보충 설명해주는 말이다.
형용사의 역할은 크게 한정적 용법과 서술적 용법으로 나눌 수 있다.

2 형용사의 한정적 용법

형용사의 한정적 용법은 형용사가 명사의 앞이나 뒤에서 직접 꾸며주는 것을 말하며, 주로 앞에서 꾸며준다.

형용사의 한정적 용법		예문
명사 앞에서 수식		She is a beautiful woman. 그녀는 아름다운 여성이다. He is a kind person. 그는 친절한 사람이다.
명사 뒤에서 수식	-thing, -body, -one으로 끝나는 명사는 뒤에서 수식	I want something special for my birthday present. 나는 생일 선물로 특별한 것을 원한다.
	형용사가 다른 어구를 동반하는 경우 뒤에서 수식	There is a box full of apples. 사과가 가득 들어 있는 상자 하나가 있다.

> **Tip**
> 관사(a, an, the)나 소유격, 또는 수를 나타내는 말은 형용사 앞에 온다.
> This is his new cap. 이것은 그의 새로운 모자이다.
> I have two beautiful rings. 나는 두 개의 아름다운 반지가 있다.

3 형용사의 서술적 용법

형용사의 서술적 용법은 동사 뒤에서 주어나 목적어를 보충 설명해 주는 것이다.

형용사의 서술적 용법	예문
동사 뒤에서 주어를 보충 설명	You look healthy. 너는 건강해 보인다.
목적어 뒤에서 목적어를 보충 설명	Her song makes me happy. 그녀의 노래는 나를 행복하게 만든다.

> **Tip**
> be, become, get, come, look, feel, sound, taste, smell 등의 동사 뒤에 오는 형용사는 주어를 보충 설명해 주는 역할을 한다.

> **Tip**
> think, find, make, keep 등의 동사가 사용된 문장에서 형용사는 목적어를 보충 설명해 주는 역할을 한다.

A 다음 괄호 안에서 알맞은 것을 고르시오.

1 Olivia has (long hair / hair long).

2 The novel is very (interesting / interestingly).

3 My grandmother has (gentle a / a gentle) smile.

4 This potato pizza tastes (delicious / deliciously).

5 She is (sad / sadly) to see the movie.

6 Emma thinks him (friend / friendly).

7 My clothes got (wet / wetly) because of the rain.

8 It's very hot. I want (something cold / cold something) to drink.

9 Heather doesn't like (old her / her old) computer.

10 There was (delicious nothing / nothing delicious) at the restaurant.

novel 소설
gentle 온화한
wet 젖다
because of ~ ~때문에
friendly 친절한

B 다음 괄호 안의 형용사를 적절한 위치에 넣어 문장을 다시 쓰시오.

1 IU is a singer. (famous)

➡ _____

2 Lucy is a student. (smart)

➡ _____

3 I need someone. (diligent)

➡ _____

4 He did an action. (dangerous)

➡ _____

5 He surprised us with his performance. (perfect)

➡ _____

famous 유명한
smart 똑똑한
diligent 부지런한, 성실한
dangerous 위험한
action 행동
perfect 완벽한
surprise 놀라게 하다
performance 공연, 연기

STEP **2**

Grammar **PRACTICE**

A 주어진 단어와 우리말을 이용하여 빈칸에 알맞은 말을 쓰시오.

1 나는 그 말을 들으니 행복을 느낀다. (happy, feel)

   ➡ I _____ _____ to hear that.

2 우리에게 정확한 정보를 알려주세요. (correct, information)

   ➡ Please tell us the _____ _____.

3 프리지아 꽃은 향기로운 냄새가 난다. (sweet, smell)

   ➡ The freesia _____ _____.

4 귀중한 액세서리는 안전한 장소에 보관하는 것이 좋겠다. (place, safe)

   ➡ You had better place your accessories in a _____ _____.

5 그 카메라에 문제가 있니? (wrong, anything)

   ➡ Is there _____ _____ with the camera?

6 그는 친구들에게 결코 거짓말을 하지 않는다. 그는 정직한 학생이다. (honest, student)

   ➡ He never lies to my friends. He is an _____ _____.

correct 정확한
information 정보
smell 냄새가 나다
sweet 달콤한, 향기로운
safe 안전한
place 장소
wrong 틀린, 잘못된
lie 거짓말을 하다

B 다음 빈칸에 적절한 말을 보기에서 골라 문장을 완성하시오. (단, 한 번씩만 쓸 것)

| 보기 | red | hungry | empty | expensive | dirty | cheerful |

1 This watch is not very _____. I will buy it.

2 Don't touch your eyes with _____ hands.

3 Mia looks great in the _____ dress.

4 Are you busy now? Could you take away the _____ bottles?

5 My teacher looks _____. She has been laughing all day.

6 I'm so _____. What do you want for lunch?

red 빨간색의
empty 비어 있는
expensive 비싼
dirty 더러운
cheerful 발랄한, 활기찬
laugh 웃다
take away 치우다

C 틀린 부분을 찾아 바르게 고쳐 문장을 다시 쓰시오.

1 There is a tree tall on the hill.

   ➡ _____

2 This fish tastes freshly.

   ➡ _____

3 She helped sick her friend yesterday.

   ➡ _____

4 His attitude made angry me.

   ➡ _____

5 We had wonderful a time.

   ➡ _____

6 The blanket keeps me warmly.

   ➡ _____

7 There was strange something in the dark.

   ➡ _____

hill 언덕
freshly 신선하게
attitude 태도
wonderful 멋진
blanket 담요
warmly 따뜻하게
strange 이상한, 낯선

D 우리말과 같은 뜻이 되도록 주어진 단어를 바르게 배열하시오.

1 그녀의 아버지는 오늘 심각해 보인다. (serious, father, looks, her, today)

   ➡ _____

2 우리는 여러 가지 색의 장미를 심었다. (of roses, many, we, colors, different, planted)

   ➡ _____

3 Wendy는 창문이 열려 있는 것을 발견했다. (the window, Wendy, open, found)

   ➡ _____

4 나는 나를 도와줄 특별한 누군가가 필요하다. (special, to help, I, me, somebody, need)

   ➡ _____

serious 심각한, 진지한
different 다른, 여러 가지의
open 열려 있는

1 다음 중 짝지어진 단어의 관계가 보기와 <u>다른</u> 것을 고르시오.

> help - helpful

① wind - windy
② wisdom - wise
③ advice - advise
④ youth - young
⑤ beauty - beautiful

2 다음 우리말과 같은 뜻이 되도록 빈칸에 들어갈 알맞은 것을 고르시오.

> 그는 주말에 특별하게 할 일이 없다.
> = He has _____ to do on weekends.

① nothing
② something special
③ special something
④ nothing special
⑤ special nothing

3 빈칸에 a를 쓸 수 <u>없는</u> 문장을 고르시오.

① That's _____ good idea.
② I'm _____ hungry now.
③ She made _____ funny face.
④ Spring is _____ warm season.
⑤ I got _____ special gift from my mom.

4 빈칸에 들어갈 수 <u>없는</u> 것을 고르시오.

> Andrea is a _____ student.

① funny
② smart
③ pretty
④ diligent
⑤ honestly

5 밑줄 친 부분이 어법상 <u>어색한</u> 것을 고르시오.

① I feel very <u>tired</u>.
② That sounds <u>good</u>.
③ This soup tastes <u>greatly</u>.
④ The song became <u>popular</u>.
⑤ Her perfume smells <u>sweet</u>.

6 주어진 단어를 이용하여 다음 우리말을 영어로 쓸 때, <u>다섯 번째</u>로 오는 것을 고르시오.

> 나는 뭔가 재미있는 것을 알고 싶다.
> (funny, want, something, know, to, I)

① to
② funny
③ want
④ something
⑤ know

7 빈칸에 들어갈 수 <u>없는</u> 말을 고르시오.

> A How does she look?
> B _____

① She looks sad.
② She looks anger.
③ She looks very happy
④ She looks really cool.
⑤ She looks a little lonely.

---

wisdom 지혜   wise 지혜로운   advise 충고하다   youth 젊음   young 어린   gift 선물   funny 재미있는   popular 인기있는   perfume 향수
anger 화, 분노   alone 외로운, 혼자의

8 다음 중 어법상 어색한 문장을 고르시오.

① Jane thinks you smart.

② Exercise keeps me healthy.

③ The movie makes us bored.

④ I found the book difficult.

⑤ Good weather makes me happily.

9 밑줄 친 부분과 쓰임이 같은 것을 고르시오.

> My grandmother has <u>weak</u> eyes.

① The man looks <u>sick</u>.

② That cloth feels <u>smooth</u>.

③ The music sounds <u>nice</u>.

④ These jeans are too <u>big</u> for me.

⑤ She has many <u>different</u> hobbies.

10 다음 두 문장이 같은 뜻이 되도록 빈칸에 들어갈 알맞은 것을 고르시오.

> The boy is very kind.
>
> = He is _____.

① very kind boy

② a very kind boy

③ very a kind boy

④ a kind very boy

⑤ a very boy kind

11 다음 중 어법상 어색한 문장을 고르시오.

① Is there anything exciting?

② I bought something special.

③ I want something deliciously.

④ There's something wrong with my phone.

⑤ She smelled something good in the kitchen.

12 다음 두 문장이 같은 뜻이 되도록 빈칸에 들어갈 알맞은 말을 쓰시오.

> The painting is amazing.
>
> = It is _____ _____ _____.

→ _____

13 어법상 어색한 부분을 찾아 바르게 고쳐 쓰시오.

> The milk smells badly.

_____ → _____

14 주어진 단어를 이용하여 다음 우리말을 영어로 쓰시오.

> 나는 어떤 다른 것을 시도해 보았다.
>
> (something, try, different)

→ _____

15 주어진 단어를 바르게 배열하여 다음 우리말을 영어로 쓰시오.

> 너는 파티에서 흥미로운 누군가를 만났니?
>
> (meet, did, interesting, at the party, you, anybody)

→ _____

_____

---

healthy 건강한 bored 지루한 difficult 어려운 happily 행복하게 weak 약한 smooth 매끄러운 hobby 취미 exciting 신나는 amazing 놀라운
badly 나쁘게, 서투르게 anybody (의문문에서) 누군가

수량형용사

1 수량형용사

수량형용사는 명사의 막연한 수나 양을 나타내는 형용사이다.

2 many, much, a lot of, lots of

many, much, a lot of, lots of는 모두 '많은'이라는 의미이며 many는 셀 수 있는 명사 앞에, much는 셀 수 없는 명사 앞에 쓴다. a lot of와 lots of는 셀 수 있는 명사와 셀 수 없는 명사 앞에 모두 쓸 수 있다.

수량 형용사	뒤에 오는 명사	예문
many	셀 수 있는 명사의 복수형	There are many people at the amusement park. 놀이공원에 많은 사람들이 있다.
much	셀 수 없는 명사	We get very much rain in summer. 여름에는 비가 많이 온다.
a lot of = lots of	셀 수 있는 명사의 복수형, 셀 수 없는 명사	I have to do a lot of homework. 나는 많은 숙제를 해야 한다. There are a lot of flowers around the school. 학교 주변에 꽃들이 많다.

3 a few, a little, few, little

a few, a little은 '약간의, 몇몇의'라는 의미이며 a few는 셀 수 있는 명사 앞에, a little은 셀 수 없는 명사 앞에 쓴다. few, little은 '거의 없는'이라는 의미이며 few는 셀 수 있는 명사 앞에, little은 셀 수 없는 명사 앞에 쓴다.

수량형용사	뒤에 오는 명사	예문
a few	셀 수 있는 명사의 복수형	Alice has a few friends. Alice는 몇 명의 친구가 있다.
few		There are few cars in the parking lot. 주차장에 자동차가 거의 없다.
a little	셀 수 없는 명사	I spread a little butter on my bread. 나는 빵에 약간의 버터를 발랐다.
little		He has little money in my wallet. 그는 지갑에 돈이 거의 없다.

4 some, any

some과 any는 '약간의, 조금의'라는 의미이며 셀 수 있는 명사와 셀 수 없는 명사 앞에 모두 쓸 수 있다.

수량형용사	문장의 종류	예문
some	긍정문	I bought some roses for you. 나는 너를 위해 장미를 좀 샀다.
any	부정문	I don't have any change. 나는 잔돈이 없다.
	의문문	Do you have any ideas? 의견 있으세요?

> **Tip**
> 권유할 때나, 긍정의 대답이 기대되는 경우에는 의문문에서도 some을 쓴다.
> Do you want some dessert? 디저트 좀 드실래요?

> **Tip**
> Any가 긍정문에 쓰일 때에는 '어떤 ~라도'의 의미를 갖는다.
> Any boy in my class knows the answer to the question. 우리 반에 어떤 소년도 그 질문에 대한 대답을 안다.

A 다음 괄호 안에서 알맞은 것을 고르시오.

1 I don't have (many / much) time to study.

2 I want to ask (a few / a little) questions to you.

3 There are (some / any) people on the subway.

4 She bought (few / a little) food at the supermarket.

5 He drinks (many / a lot of) milk every morning.

6 I can learn (many / much) interesting things there.

7 There were (lots of / much) animals in the zoo.

8 Do you have (some / any) plans for Children's Day?

9 Chris made (a few / a little) mistakes in his speech.

10 There are (few / a few) people in the office. It's almost empty.

subway 지하철
Children's Day 어린이날
mistake 실수
speech 연설
almost 거의
office 사무실
empty 비어 있는

B much와 many 중 밑줄 친 부분과 바꿔 쓸 수 있는 것을 쓰시오.

1 It contains <u>a lot of</u> useful information. _____

2 The vegetable has <u>lots of</u> nutrients. _____

3 Jessica has <u>a lot of</u> knowledge about classical music. _____

4 My teacher gave me <u>a lot of</u> advice. _____

5 My grandpa has <u>lots of</u> trouble reading my small handwriting. _____

6 This December is very cold with <u>a lot of</u> snow. _____

7 There are <u>a lot of</u> cars in the parking lot. _____

8 My hobby is collecting <u>lots of</u> stamps from around the world. _____

contain 포함하다
useful 유용한
nutrient 영양소
knowledge 지식
parking lot 주차장
collect 모으다, 수집하다
stamp 우표

A 주어진 우리말을 이용하여 빈칸에 알맞은 말을 쓰시오.

valley 계곡
refrigerator 냉장고
nowadays 요즘
more 더 많은

1 그 계곡에는 물이 거의 없다.

➡ There was _____ _____ in the valley.

2 며칠 전에 나는 너에게 전화했었다.

➡ _____ _____ days ago, I called you.

3 그는 아이스크림을 좀 살 것이다.

➡ He will _____ _____ ice cream.

4 냉장고에 주스 좀 있나요?

➡ Is there _____ _____ in the refrigerator?

5 나는 요즘 여가 시간이 거의 없다.

➡ I _____ _____ free time nowadays.

6 당신은 남동생이 있나요?

➡ Do you _____ _____ brothers?

7 케이크 좀 더 드시겠어요?

➡ Do you _____ _____ more cake?

B 다음 빈칸에 알맞은 말을 보기에서 골라 쓰시오. (단, 한 번씩만 쓸 것)

England 영국
breakfast 아침식사

| 보기 | any | many | a little | some | much |

1 Would you like _____ tea?

2 I don't have _____ friends in England.

3 I drank too _____ coffee today, so I can't sleep.

4 How _____ hours a day do you watch a TV?

5 I ate _____ breakfast. So I'm hungry now.

C 밑줄 친 부분을 바르게 고쳐 문장을 다시 쓰시오.

1 She adds <u>a few</u> sugar to the food.

   ➡ _____

2 Could you lend me <u>any</u> money?

   ➡ _____

3 She has too <u>many</u> furniture in her room. (한 단어로)

   ➡ _____

4 The road was covered with <u>a few</u> ice.

   ➡ _____

5 <u>Much</u> kangaroos live in Australia. (한 단어로)

   ➡ _____

6 There were <u>little</u> people at the party.

   ➡ _____

7 I have <u>few</u> knowledge of computers.

   ➡ _____

sugar 설탕
lend 빌려주다
furniture 가구
be covered with ~
~으로 뒤덮인

D 우리말과 같은 뜻이 되도록 주어진 단어를 바르게 배열하시오. (단, 알맞은 수량형용사를 넣을 것)

1 우리는 가을에 많은 단풍잎을 볼 수 있다. (can, maple leaves, we, in fall, see)

   ➡ _____

2 그는 샌드위치에 햄을 거의 넣지 않았다. (ham, put, he, on his sandwich)

   ➡ _____

3 나는 고궁에서 많은 사진을 찍었다. (I, at the old palace, pictures, took)

   ➡ _____

4 Amy는 저녁으로 약간의 피자를 먹었다. (pizza, Amy, for dinner, ate)

   ➡ _____

maple leaf 단풍잎
palace 궁전
take a picture 사진을 찍다

1 빈칸에 들어갈 수 <u>없는</u> 것을 고르시오.

> We have a few _____ .

① water ② cameras ③ pencils
④ bottles ⑤ questions

2 밑줄 친 부분과 바꿔 쓸 수 있는 것을 고르시오.

> Does Helen do <u>a lot of</u> exercise?

① many ② much ③ a few
④ few ⑤ lot of

3 다음 우리말과 같은 뜻이 되도록 빈칸에 들어갈 알맞은 것을 고르시오.

> 농장에는 몇 마리의 동물들이 있다.
> = There are _____ animals on the farm.

① few ② a few ③ little
④ a little ⑤ any

4 빈칸에 들어갈 수 <u>없는</u> 것을 고르시오.

> _____ people made reservations at a hotel.

① Few ② A few ③ A little
④ A lot of ⑤ Many

5 빈칸에 공통으로 들어갈 알맞은 것을 고르시오.

> • Do you want _____ more meat?
> • There are _____ hats in the store.

① any ② few ③ much
④ some ⑤ lot of

[6-7] 빈칸에 들어갈 말이 순서대로 바르게 짝지어진 것을 고르시오.

6

> • It made _____ noise in the forest.
> • There are _____ rivers in the city.
> • He has _____ friends at school.

① few - little - a few
② a few - few - a little
③ a little - few - little
④ a little - little - few
⑤ little - a few - few

7

> My mom eats _____ fruits every day, and I eat _____ cheese.

① many - many
② much - much
③ many - a lot of
④ much - many
⑤ lots of - a lot

---

exercise 운동 farm 농장 make a reservation 예약하다 meat 고기 hat 모자 noise 소음 forest 숲 river 강 fruit 과일

8 빈칸에 들어갈 말이 바르게 짝지어진 것을 고르시오.

> A Is there _____ orange juice?
>
> B Yes, there is _____ orange juice on the table.

① any - some
② any - many
③ few - much
④ some - many
⑤ much - few

9 빈칸에 a little을 쓸 수 없는 것을 고르시오.

① We have _____ food.
② He had _____ ideas about it.
③ Add _____ pepper and salt.
④ Give me _____ butter and jam.
⑤ There is _____ garbage in the room.

10 빈칸에 '많은'이라는 뜻의 한 단어를 넣을 때 들어갈 말이 나머지와 다른 것을 고르시오.

① He bought me _____ flowers.
② My little sister has _____ dolls.
③ I have to drink _____ water a day.
④ How _____ days are there in a week?
⑤ There are _____ children in the park.

11 다음 중 어법상 어색한 문장을 고르시오.

① I took some pills for the flu.
② She'll be back in few days.
③ My brother ate many cookies.
④ I need a lot of information about it.
⑤ The country produces many apples.

12 다음 두 문장이 같은 뜻이 되도록 빈칸에 들어갈 알맞은 말을 쓰시오.

> Her coat has many buttons.
>
> = Her coat has _____ _____ buttons.

→ _____

13 어법상 어색한 부분을 찾아 바르게 고쳐 쓰시오. (단, 한 단어로 쓸 것)

> There are much languages in the world.

_____ → _____

14 다음 문장을 부정문으로 바꾸시오.

> I have some plans for this weekend.

→ _____
_____

15 주어진 단어를 바르게 배열하여 다음 우리말을 영어로 쓰시오.

> 나는 그곳에서 많은 오래된 나무들과 야생 동물들을 보았다.
>
> (old, there, wild animals, saw, and, I, many, trees)

→ _____
_____

---

pepper 후추 garbage 쓰레기 doll 인형 pill 알약 produce 생산하다 button 단추 language 언어

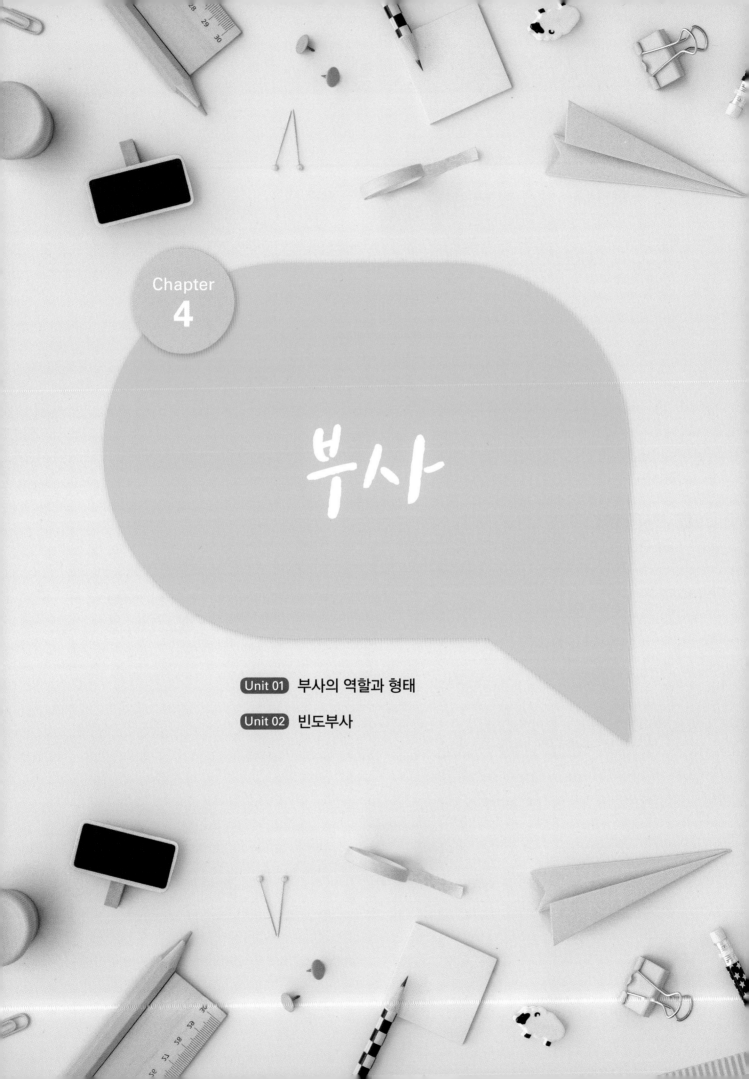

Chapter
4

부사

부사의 역할과 형태

1 부사의 역할

부사는 문장에서 동사, 형용사, 다른 부사, 또는 문장 전체를 꾸며주는 말이다.

부사의 역할	예문
동사 수식	He drove slowly. 그는 천천히 운전한다.
형용사 수식	I feel very happy. 나는 매우 행복하다.
부사 수식	The bus passed very quickly. 버스가 매우 빨리 지나갔다.
문장 전체 수식	Fortunately, the weather cleared up. 다행히도, 날씨가 갰다.

2 부사의 형태

부사는 주로 형용사에 -ly를 붙여서 만드는데, 다음과 같은 규칙이 있다. 대체로 '〜하게'라고 해석한다.

형용사	변화 규칙	부사
대부분의 형용사	형용사 + -ly	badly, slowly, heavily, safely, softly, warmly, kindly, carefully, quickly, beautifully, strongly
자음 + -y로 끝나는 형용사	y를 i로 바꾸고 + -ly	happily, easily, lazily, angrily, busily
예외	형용사 = 부사	high 높은/높게, late 늦은/늦게, early 이른/일찍, fast 빠른/빨리, hard 어려운/열심히, well 건강한/잘, pretty 귀여운/매우

We have to handle it carefully. 우리는 그것을 조심스럽게 다뤄야 해.
I found my missing bag easily. 나는 잃어버린 가방을 쉽게 찾았다.

3 주의해야 할 부사

형용사와 형태가 같은 부사에 -ly를 붙이면 전혀 다른 뜻의 부사가 되기도 하고, -ly로 끝나지만 형용사인 경우도 있다.

주의해야 할 부사	형용사와 형태가 같은 부사 + -ly → 전혀 다른 뜻의 부사	late 늦게 → lately 최근에, hard 열심히 → hardly 거의 ~ 않다, near 가까이 → nearly 거의, high 높게 → highly 매우, 대단히
	-ly로 끝나는 형용사	lovely 사랑스러운, lonely 외로운, silly 어리석은, friendly 친절한, ugly 못생긴, weekly 매주의, monthly 매달의, elderly 나이 든

Grammar START

A 다음 형용사의 부사형을 쓰시오.

1 exact ➡ _____

2 fair ➡ _____

3 honest ➡ _____

4 general ➡ _____

5 severe ➡ _____

6 thorough ➡ _____

7 strange ➡ _____

8 certain ➡ _____

9 sweet ➡ _____

10 particular ➡ _____

11 clear ➡ _____

12 early ➡ _____

13 individual ➡ _____

14 fast ➡ _____

15 glad ➡ _____

16 different ➡ _____

17 special ➡ _____

18 smooth ➡ _____

19 similar ➡ _____

20 fortunate ➡ _____

exact 정확한
fair 공정한
honest 정직한
general 일반적인
severe 심각한
thorough 빈틈없는
strange 이상한
certain 확실한
particular 특정한
clear 분명한
early 이른
individual 개인의, 각각의
glad 기쁜
different 어려운
special 특별한
smooth 부드러운
similar 비슷한
fortunate 운 좋은, 다행인

B 밑줄 친 부사가 꾸며주는 부분을 찾아 동그라미 치시오.

1 John eats so fast.

2 Jasmine speaks English fluently.

3 Suddenly, the phone rang.

4 I have to practice yoga hard.

5 Richard's mother is pretty young.

6 Finally, we won the game.

7 Thank you so much.

8 The woman dances beautifully.

fluently 유창하게
suddenly 갑자기
ring 울리다
practice 연습하다
pretty 꽤, 상당히
finally 마침내

A   두 문장의 의미가 같도록 빈칸에 알맞은 부사를 쓰시오.

1   Tom is a fast runner.

= Tom runs _____.

2   Daniel is a slow walker.

= Daniel walks _____.

3   Sally is a careful thinker.

= Sally thinks _____.

4   Joe is a precise proofreader.

= Joe proofreads _____.

5   Chris is a sharp questioner.

= Chris questions _____.

6   Ann is an active volunteer.

= Ann volunteers _____.

careful 주의 깊은
precise 꼼꼼한
proofreader 교정자
question 질문하다
sharp 예리한, 선명한
active 활동적인, 적극적인
volunteer
자원봉사자, 자원봉사를 하다

B   주어진 단어와 우리말을 이용하여 빈칸에 알맞은 말을 쓰시오. (시제에 유의할 것)

1   사자가 큰 소리로 으르렁거리고 있었다. (roar, loud)

➡ The lion was _____ _____.

2   Alice는 그 일을 잘했니? (do, nice)

➡ Did Alice _____ the work _____?

3   Cathy는 그때 현명하게 행동했다. (act, wise)

➡ Cathy _____ _____ at that time.

4   그 야구팀은 경기에서 쉽게 승리했다. (win, easy)

➡ The baseball team _____ the game _____.

5   Brian은 항상 부드럽게 말한다. (speak, soft)

➡ Brian always _____ _____.

roar 으르렁거리다
at that time 그때

C 밑줄 친 부분을 바르게 고쳐 문장을 다시 쓰시오.

1 It hard rained this summer.

   ➡ _____

2 Sarah is a well friendly girl.

   ➡ _____

3 The bird is flying highly in the sky.

   ➡ _____

4 The subway came 15 minutes lately.

   ➡ _____

5 Kelly closed the window quiet.

   ➡ _____

6 I tried hardly to get a good grade.

   ➡ _____

7 He is so busily. I will meet him the next time.

   ➡ _____

hardly 거의 ~ 않다
friendly 친절한, 상냥한
quiet 조용한
grade 성적

D 우리말과 같은 뜻이 되도록 주어진 단어를 바르게 배열하시오.

1 밖에 바람이 강하게 불고 있다. (blowing, outside, the wind, is, strongly)

   ➡ _____

2 너는 위험하게 운전하면 안 된다. (drive, you, not, dangerously, must)

   ➡ _____

3 나는 너를 거의 이해할 수가 없다. (you, I, understand, hardly, can)

   ➡ _____

4 지원자들은 거의 모두 여자들이었다. (all, were, women, nearly, the applicants)

   ➡ _____

blow (바람이) 불다
nearly 거의
applicant 지원자

1 짝지어진 단어의 관계가 나머지와 <u>다른</u> 것을 고르시오.

① easy - easily   ② real - really

③ heavy - heavily   ④ final - finally

⑤ friend - friendly

2 형용사와 부사의 관계가 <u>잘못</u> 짝지어진 것을 고르시오.

① safe - safely   ② lazy - lazily

③ honest - honestly ④ well - welly

⑤ happy - happily

3 빈칸에 들어갈 말이 바르게 짝지어진 것을 고르시오.

> • Don't eat so _____. We still have time.
>
> • Please speak _____.

① fastly - slow

② fast - slowly

③ fastly - slowly

④ fast - slow

⑤ fastly - slowness

4 빈칸에 들어갈 수 <u>없는</u> 것을 고르시오.

> I carry the box _____.

① lovely   ② safely   ③ slowly

④ easily   ⑤ carefully

5 다음 우리말과 같은 뜻이 되도록 빈칸에 들어갈 알맞은 것을 고르시오.

> 나는 그의 메시지를 늦게 확인했다. 나는 그에게 빨리 전화를 해야 한다.
>
> = I checked his message _____. I should call him _____.

① late - quick   ② lately - quickly

③ late - quickly   ④ lately - quick

⑤ late - quicken

6 다음 두 문장이 같은 뜻이 되도록 빈칸에 알맞은 것을 고르시오.

> Jason is a good actor.
>
> = Jason acts _____.

① right   ② nice   ③ bad

④ great   ⑤ well

[7-8] 밑줄 친 부분의 품사가 나머지와 <u>다른</u> 것을 고르시오.

7 ① I don't feel so <u>lonely</u>.

② My English class has a <u>weekly</u> test.

③ The <u>silly</u> woman lost all her money.

④ He always speaks <u>softly</u> and carefully.

⑤ An <u>elderly</u> man is walking on the street.

---

safely 안전하게 lazily 게으르게 honestly 정직하게 safely 안전하게 slowly 천천히 easily 쉽게 carefully 조심스럽게 late 늦게 lately 최근에
quick 빠른 quickly 빨리 softly 부드럽게 elderly 나이가 든

8
① I'm truly sorry about that.
② I went to bed early last night.
③ Alice always worked perfectly.
④ She ordered a free monthly catalog.
⑤ The plane is flying high in the sky.

9 밑줄 친 단어의 의미가 보기와 같은 것을 고르시오.

> He does exercise very hard every morning.

① This bed is too hard.
② I'm tired from my hard work.
③ They trained hard in Japan.
④ It is hard to start a new job.
⑤ She had a hard time finishing the report.

10 밑줄 친 부분과 쓰임이 같은 것을 고르시오.

> It is quite warm today.

① He suddenly changed his mind.
② Finally, I arrived at the hospital.
③ I especially like baseball very much.
④ She solved the math problem differently.
⑤ The restaurant on the corner is pretty good.

11 밑줄 친 부분이 어법상 어색한 것을 고르시오.
① He leaves exactly in an hour.
② She closed the door quietly.
③ Brian sang a song so loudly.
④ You didn't try hardly on this exam.
⑤ He should think a little more carefully.

12 다음 두 문장이 같은 뜻이 되도록 빈칸에 들어갈 알맞은 말을 쓰시오.

> She is a clear thinker.
> = She thinks _____.

→ _____

[13-14] 다음 문장에서 어법상 어색한 부분을 찾아 바르게 고쳐 쓰시오.

13
> They are preparing for the event busy.

_____ → _____

14
> Luck, they arrived at the station in time.

_____ → _____

15 주어진 단어를 바르게 배열하여 다음 우리말을 영어로 쓰시오.

> Mark는 기타를 꽤 잘 친다.
> (plays, well, guitar, Mark, quite, the)

→ _____

truly 진심으로 train 훈련 받다 have a hard time -ing ~하는 데 힘든 시간을 보내다 clear 냉철한, 또렷한 think 생각하다, 사고하다 prepare 준비하다 especially 특히 differently 다르게 exactly 정확히 quite 꽤, 상당히 quietly 조용히

빈도부사

1 빈도부사의 종류

어떤 일의 빈번한 정도나 횟수를 나타내는 부사를 빈도부사라고 한다. 빈도부사는 빈도수에 따라 다음과 같은 순서이다.

빈도부사	예문
always 항상	He is always late. 그는 항상 늦는다.
usually 보통, 대개	They usually go to school by bus. 그들은 보통 버스를 타고 학교에 간다.
often 자주, 종종	My family often has dinner together. 우리 가족은 자주 저녁을 함께 먹는다.
sometimes 가끔, 때때로	My mom sometimes makes me pasta. 엄마는 가끔씩 나에게 파스타를 만들어 주신다.
seldom 거의 ~ 않는	My sister seldom drinks coffee. 우리 언니는 커피를 거의 마시지 않는다.
never 결코 ~ 않는	I never eat fast food. 나는 결코 패스트푸드를 먹지 않는다.

2 빈도부사의 위치

빈도부사는 문장 내에서 be동사나 조동사 뒤, 일반동사 앞에 위치한다.

빈도부사의 위치	예문
be동사 뒤	His parents are always busy. 그의 부모님은 항상 바쁘셨다.
일반동사 앞	She never eats cucumbers. 그녀는 오이를 절대로 먹지 않는다.
조동사와 본동사 사이	I will often clean my room starting tomorrow. 나는 내일부터 내 방을 자주 청소할 것이다.

3 빈도를 묻는 의문문

의문문에서 빈도부사는 주어 뒤에 위치한다.

A Is he sometimes late for school? 그는 종종 학교에 늦니?

B No, he isn't. He is usually early. 아니. 그는 보통 일찍 가.

A Do you often exercise? 너는 자주 운동하니?

B Yes, I do. 응.

> **TIP**
> 어떤 동작의 빈도를 물을 때 'How often ~?'을 쓸 수 있다.
> A: How often do you go camping? 너는 얼마나 자주 캠핑을 가니?
> B: I go camping twice a month. 한 달에 두 번 가.

Grammar **START**

A 다음 괄호 안에서 알맞은 것을 고르시오.

1 Eric (always is / is always) kind.

2 Heather (often has / has often) breakfast.

3 They (are never / never are) rude to their parents.

4 Danielle (goes sometimes / sometimes goes) to bed at 12.

5 He (will usually stay / usually will stay) at home.

6 My friends (use never / never use) bad language.

7 You (always can / can always) use my computer.

8 I (seldom go / go seldom) to the movies.

9 Lily (sometimes catches / catches sometimes) a cold in winter.

10 Does she (study usually / usually study) 2 hours a day?

catch a cold 감기에 걸리다
rude 무례한, 버릇없는
bad language
나쁜 말, 욕설

B 다음 문장에서 빈도부사를 찾아 쓰고, 엄마를 자주 도와드리는 사람부터 이름을 쓰시오.

1 Nari never helps Mom after school.   ➡ _____

2 Mina always helps Mom after school.   ➡ _____

3 Juho seldom helps Mom after school.   ➡ _____

4 Seho sometimes helps Mom after school.   ➡ _____

5 Jina often helps Mom after school.   ➡ _____

6 _____ ➡ _____ ➡ _____ ➡ _____ ➡ _____

Grammar **PRACTICE**

A 보기와 같이 주어진 빈도부사가 들어갈 알맞은 위치에 V표 하시오.

> 보기 Sally ✓ walks to school. (always)

1 I wash the dishes. (sometimes)

2 They talk about books. (usually)

3 David will watch TV on weekends. (never)

4 Mia plays the piano. (often)

5 She is polite to others. (always)

6 He can play computer games. (sometimes)

7 Cathy reads the newspaper. (seldom)

8 Does she visit her grandparents? (often)

9 Alice skips breakfast on weekdays. (usually)

wash the dishes
설거지를 하다
weekend 주말
polite 예의 바른, 공손한
newspaper 신문
grandparents 조부모
skip 거르다, 빼다
weekday 평일

B 밑줄 친 부분을 어법상 바르게 고쳐 쓰시오.

1 They speak never loudly. ➡ _____

2 She often is late for appointments. ➡ _____

3 I go seldom to the hospital. ➡ _____

4 He always is happy. ➡ _____

5 Sam goes usually to bed at 10. ➡ _____

6 I never will change my mind. ➡ _____

7 He eats never out on weekends. ➡ _____

8 Mike always will invite Sue. ➡ _____

9 My mom uses usually her credit card. ➡ _____

appointment 약속
change 바꾸다
mind 마음, 생각
eat out 외식하다
invite 초대하다
credit card 신용카드

C 괄호 안의 단어를 넣어 문장을 다시 쓰시오.

1 My sisters do their homework together. (always)

➡ _____

2 I visit the museum with my friends. (often)

➡ _____

3 My brother cleans his room on weekends. (never)

➡ _____

4 I go to the library with my dad. (sometimes)

➡ _____

5 My family and I can ride a horse on Saturdays. (usually)

➡ _____

6 They were tired and hungry after school. (often)

➡ _____

museum 박물관
library 도서관
ride 타다
horse 말

D 우리말과 같은 뜻이 되도록 주어진 단어를 바르게 배열하시오.

1 나는 가끔 부모님과 함께 영화를 본다.
   (sometimes, parents, movies, I watch, my, with)

➡ _____

2 나는 보통 아빠와 함께 옷을 사러 간다.
   (with my dad, usually, go shopping, for clothes, I)

➡ _____

3 나는 자주 엄마와 함께 김밥을 만든다. (with my mom, gimbap, make, often, I)

➡ _____

4 나는 항상 가족과 함께 공원을 산책한다.
   (always, with my family, in the park, I, take a walk)

➡ _____

go shopping
쇼핑하러 가다
take a walk 산책하다

1 빈칸에 들어갈 수 <u>없는</u> 것을 고르시오.

> We _____ have dinner together.

① often   ② always   ③ never
④ sometime   ⑤ seldom

2 다음 중 usually가 들어갈 알맞은 곳을 고르시오.

> They ① go ② hiking ③ on ④ weekends ⑤.

3 빈칸에 들어갈 수 <u>없는</u> 것을 고르시오.

> A   How often do you exercise a week?
> B   I _____ exercise.

① never   ② usually   ③ already
④ always   ⑤ often

4 다음 우리말과 같은 뜻이 되도록 빈칸에 들어갈 알맞은 것을 고르시오.

> 나는 저녁에는 거의 커피를 마시지 않는다.
> = I _____ have coffee at night.

① never   ② always   ③ usually
④ sometimes   ⑤ seldom

5 다음 우리말을 영어로 바르게 옮긴 것을 고르시오.

> 너는 보통 시험 보기 전에 긴장하니?

① Do you often nervous before tests?
② Are you seldom nervous before tests?
③ Are usually you nervous before tests?
④ Are you usually nervous before tests?
⑤ Are you sometimes nervous before tests?

6 빈칸에 들어갈 말이 바르게 짝지어진 것을 고르시오.

> I _____ go to bed early, so I am
> _____ late for school.

① never - never
② often - always
③ always - never
④ never - seldom
⑤ always - usually

7 빈칸에 들어갈 알맞은 것을 고르시오.

> A   Why don't you eat pizza for lunch?
> B   No, thanks. I _____ eat pizza. It is not good for my health.

① like   ② always   ③ love
④ often   ⑤ never

---

dinner 저녁 식사   go hiking 하이킹을 가다   exercise 운동하다   nervous 긴장한, 불안해하는   Why don't you ~? ~하는 게 어때?   health 건강

8 다음 우리말과 같은 뜻이 되도록 주어진 단어를 배열할 때 세 번째로 오는 것을 고르시오.

우리 아빠는 항상 나를 학교에 데려다 주신다.

(takes, school, always, father, me, to, my)

① always   ② took   ③ to
④ me   ⑤ school

9 빈칸에 들어갈 말로 알맞은 것을 고르시오.

A How often do you go on trips?
B _____

① I like going on trips.
② I sometimes go on trips.
③ I go on trips with my parents.
④ I went on a trip last month.
⑤ I will go on a trip to Hawaii.

10 밑줄 친 부분이 어법상 어색한 것을 고르시오.

① I never tell lies.
② I often watch soccer games.
③ He sometimes played with his dog.
④ We play usually basketball at the park.
⑤ She always buys books at the bookstore.

11 다음 중 어법상 어색한 문장을 고르시오.

① We will never give up.
② I often am home by 8 o'clock.
③ She always comes home early.
④ I usually read fashion magazines.
⑤ I seldom go shopping with my friends.

[12-13] 어법상 어색한 부분을 찾아 바르게 고쳐 쓰시오.

12

Jane and I do often a lot of things together.

_____ → _____

13

You always should remember to look both way at the crosswalk.

_____ → _____

[14-15] 주어진 단어를 바르게 배열하여 다음 우리말을 영어로 쓰시오.

14

나의 여동생은 종종 그녀의 숙제를 하느라 바쁘다.

(doing, busy, is, her homework, my sister, often)

→ _____

_____

15

너는 항상 선생님 말씀을 잘 들어야 한다.

(must, carefully, listen to, always, your teacher, you)

→ _____

go on a trip 여행을 가다   Hawaii 하와이   tell a lie 거짓말하다   bookstore 서점   fashion magazine 패션 잡지   remember 기억하다
crosswalk 횡단보도   both 양쪽의   carefully 조심스럽게

1 짝지어진 단어의 관계가 보기와 <u>다른</u> 것을 고르시오.

> kind - kindly

① bad - badly
② safe - safely
③ busy - busily
④ week - weekly
⑤ strong - strongly

[2-3] 빈칸에 들어갈 알맞은 것을 고르시오.

2

> We have _____ food to eat.

① a   ② few   ③ many
④ little   ⑤ a few

3

> _____, the police could catch the thief.

① Luck   ② Lucks   ③ Luckily
④ Lucky   ⑤ Lucking

4 밑줄 친 부분의 쓰임이 나머지와 <u>다른</u> 것을 고르시오.
① It's <u>so</u> hot outside.
② I can <u>always</u> help them.
③ He lived alone and felt <u>lonely</u>.
④ She comes in 1 hour <u>late</u> on Monday morning.
⑤ <u>Generally</u>, winter is from December to February.

5 빈칸에 들어갈 수 <u>없는</u> 것을 고르시오.

> She brought a few _____ to the kitchen.

① sugar   ② apples   ③ cups
④ bottles   ⑤ bowls

6 주어진 단어를 이용하여 다음 우리말을 영어로 쓰시오.

> 나는 재미있는 것을 듣고 싶다.
>
> (hear, funny, something)

➡ _____

7 빈칸에 들어갈 말이 바르게 짝지어진 것을 고르시오.

> 그녀는 공부를 매우 열심히 했기 때문에 시험 문제를 빨리 풀었다.
>
> = She solved the questions _____ because she studied very _____.

① late - hardly   ② fastly - hard
③ fastly - hardly   ④ fast - hard
⑤ fast - hardly

8 다음 우리말을 영어로 바르게 옮긴 것을 고르시오.

> 그녀는 나이에 비해 매우 침착한 소녀이다.

① She be a high calmly girl for her age.
② She is a high calm girl for her age.
③ She is a highly calm girl for her age.
④ She is a high calmly girl for her age.
⑤ She is a highly calmly girl for her age.

9 빈칸에 들어갈 말이 바르게 짝지어진 것을 고르시오.

> • 나는 많은 사람들과 대화하려고 노력한다.
>   = I try to talk with _____ people.
>
> • 당신을 위한 좋은 소식이 좀 있어요.
>   = I have _____ good news for you.

① many - any
② many - some
③ much - some
④ much - any
⑤ much - a lot of

10 빈칸에 공통으로 들어갈 알맞은 것을 고르시오.

> • We saw _____ pictures in the gallery.
> • They threw away _____ trash in the stadium.

① Few
② little
③ much
④ many
⑤ a lot of

11 다음 중 어법상 올바른 문장을 고르시오.

① I have often time for myself.
② They will be able to leave easily.
③ She smiled happy by his looks.
④ We hope our plans go good.
⑤ You should not submit it lately.

12 주어진 단어를 바르게 배열하여 다음 우리말을 영어로 쓰시오.

> 그는 길에 약간의 동전을 떨어뜨렸다.
>
> (dropped, he, coins, on the street, a few)

➡ _____

13 밑줄 친 부분이 어법상 어색한 것을 고르시오.

① I usually wear a long skirt.
② I never go to the coffee shop.
③ I often go fishing with my dad.
④ They always play badminton.
⑤ We seldom can go on picnics.

[14-15] 다음 John의 스케줄 표를 참고하여, 조건에 맞는 말을 한 문장으로 쓰시오.

Time	7:30 a.m.	8:00 p.m.
Things to Do	read the newspaper	walk his dog
Frequency	four times a week	two times a week

> 보기   always   usually   sometimes   never

> 조건   1. 보기에서 빈도부사를 골라 사용하시오.
>   2. 주어와 동사를 갖춘 완전한 문장으로 쓰시오.

14 _____ at 7:30 a.m.

15 _____ at 8:00 p.m.

기초 탄탄 2
GRAMMAR

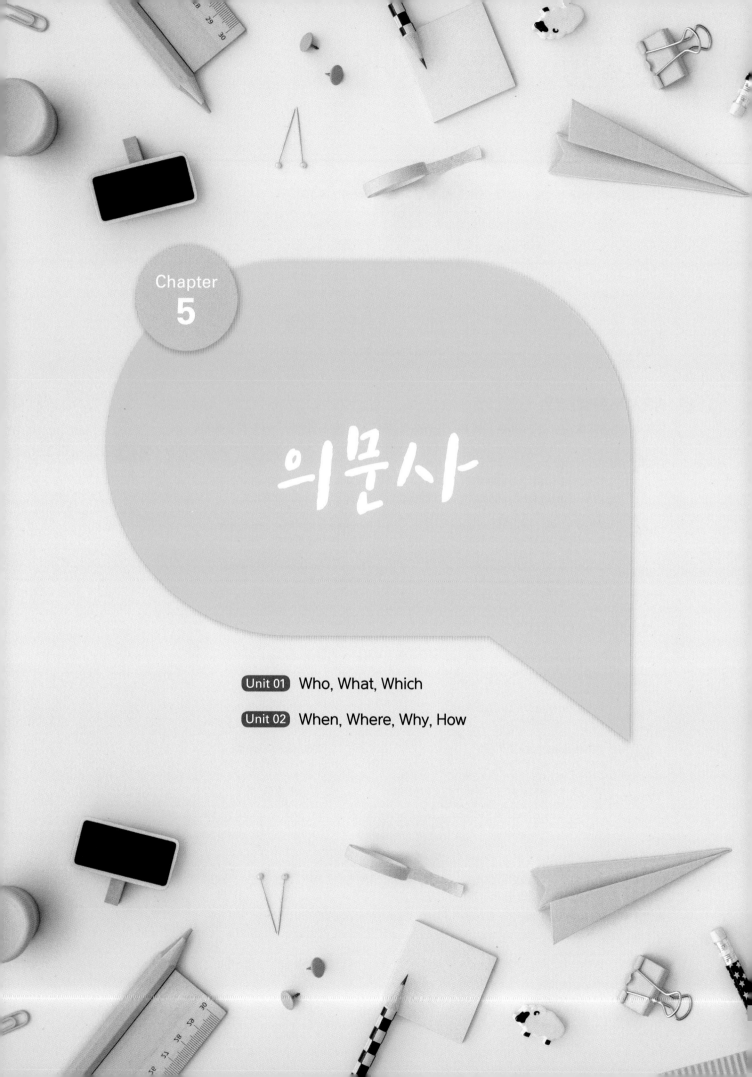

Chapter 5

의문사

1 의문사

의문사는 '누가, 언제, 무엇을, 어디서, 어떻게, 왜' 등을 물을 때 사용하는 말이다.

	Who	What	Which
의미	누구, 누가	무엇, 무슨	어느 것, 어떤
쓰임	사람에 관련된 내용을 물을 때	사람, 사물의 이름이나 직업을 물을 때	정해진 범위나 대상 중에서 어떤 것을 물을 때 사용
분류	의문대명사	의문대명사, 의문형용사	의문대명사, 의문형용사
공통점	Yes나 No로 대답하지 않고, 구체적인 내용으로 대답		

2 의문사가 주어인 경우

의문사가 주어일 때에는 의문사 바로 뒤에 동사와 와서 『의문사 + be동사/일반동사 ~?』의 형태이다.

의문사	질문	대답
Who	Who is Jane? 누가 Jane이니? Who washed the dishes? 누가 설거지했니?	Jane is that girl. Jane은 저 소녀야. Mary did it. Mary가 했어.
What	What is your favorite subject? 무엇이 네가 가장 좋아하는 과목이니?	Science is my favorite subject. 과학이 내가 가장 좋아하는 과목이야
Which	Which is my cellphone? 어느 것이 내 휴대폰이니?	The one on the left is yours. 왼쪽 게 네 것이야.

> **TiP**
> 의문사가 주어일 때,
> 의문사는 단수 취급하기
> 때문에 단수 동사를
> 써야 한다.

3 의문사가 목적어인 경우

의문사가 목적어일 때에는 『의문사 + do/does + 주어 + 동사원형 ~?』의 형태이다.

의문사	질문	대답
Who	Who did you visit yesterday? 너는 어제 누구를 방문했니?	I visited my grandparents yesterday. 나는 어제 조부모님을 방문했어.
What	What does your cat eat? 너의 고양이는 무엇을 먹니?	My cat eats fish. 내 고양이는 생선을 먹어.
Which	Which do you want, coke or orange juice? 콜라와 오렌지 주스 중에 어느 것을 원하니?	Coke, please. 콜라 주세요.

4 의문형용사

What, Which는 위와 같이 의문대명사는 물론, 명사 앞에서 형용사처럼 쓰여 '무슨(어떤) ~'라는 뜻의 의문형용사로도 쓰인다.
What과 달리 Which는 선택의 범위가 제한되어 있다.

A What drinks do you like the most? 너는 무슨 음료를 가장 좋아하니?

B I like cider the most. 나는 사이다를 가장 좋아해.

A Which tea do you like more, herb or jasmine? 허브 차와 재스민 차 중에 어떤 차를 좋아하니?

B I like Jasmine tea more. 나는 재스민 차를 더 좋아해.

> **TiP**
> '누구의'라는 의미로 소유 관계를
> 물을 때, whose를 쓸 수 있다.
> A: Whose cellphone is this?
> 이것은 누구의 휴대폰이니?
> B: It's John's.
> 그것은 John의 것이야.

Grammar START

A 다음 괄호 안에서 알맞은 것을 고르시오.

1 (Who / What) did you eat for lunch?

2 (What / Which) are you doing now?

3 (What / Which) did you buy, the coat or the cardigan?

4 (Who / What) chose this song?

5 (Who / Whose) notebook computer is that?

6 (What / Which) is your favorite color?

7 (Who / What) is that girl with the yellow dress?

8 (What / Which) did you tell your mom?

9 (Who / What) sport does he play?

10 (What / Which) do you like more, Japanese food or Chinese food?

cardigan 카디건
chose
(choose 고른다)의 과거
Japanese 일본의
Chinese 중국의
better 더 좋은

B 주어진 단어와 우리말을 이용하여 빈칸에 알맞은 말을 쓰시오.

1 너는 무슨 방법을 사용했니? (method)

➡ _____ _____ did you use?

2 너는 주말에 무엇을 하니? (do)

➡ _____ _____ you do on weekends?

3 누가 그 바나나를 먹었니? (eat)

➡ _____ _____ the banana?

4 그녀는 뭐라고 말했니? (do)

➡ _____ _____ she say?

5 너는 아침에 몇 시에 일어나니? (time)

➡ _____ _____ do you get up?

method 방법
get up 일어나다

A   대화를 읽고, 빈칸에 알맞은 의문사를 쓰시오.

1   A _____ month is it?

　　B It's May.

2   A _____ does your father do?

　　B He is a reporter.

3   A _____ did you go with there?

　　B I went there with my aunt.

4   A _____ ring is this?

　　B It's Wendy's.

5   A _____ season do you like the most?

　　B I like fall the most.

6   A _____ plays the cello?

　　B Rachel does.

7   A _____ animal do you prefer, dogs or cats?

　　B Dogs.

8   A _____ is the boy with your mom?

　　B He is my brother.

reporter 기자
aunt 이모, 고모
fall 가을
cello 첼로
prefer 더 좋아하다

B   빈칸에 들어갈 알맞은 말을 보기에서 골라 쓰시오. (단, 한 번씩만 쓸 것)

보기	What	Who	Which	Whose

1   _____ food do you like?

2   _____ made this paper doll?

3   _____ idea was that?

4   _____ does he like more, chocolate or candy?

C 틀린 부분을 찾아 바르게 고쳐 문장을 다시 쓰시오.

ping-pong 탁구
mean 의미하다
park 주차하다
person 사람, 개인

1 Which is he studying now?

    ➡ _____

2 What activity do you like, ping-pong or badminton?

    ➡ _____

3 Who are the person standing at the bus stop?

    ➡ _____

4 Which does pansori mean?

    ➡ _____

5 Who is the new teacher's name?

    ➡ _____

6 Which parked the car next to my bike?

    ➡ _____

7 Who book is this?

    ➡ _____

D 우리말과 같은 뜻이 되도록 주어진 단어를 바르게 배열하시오.

future 미래의
dream 꿈

1 공항에서 누구를 봤니? (did, at the airport, who, see, you)

    ➡ _____

2 너의 장래 꿈은 무엇이니? (future, is, dream, what, your)

    ➡ _____

3 네가 가장 좋아하는 배우는 누구니? (is, actor, your, who, favorite)

    ➡ _____

4 이것은 누구의 컵이니? (is, whose, this, cup)

    ➡ _____

[1-2] 빈칸에 들어갈 알맞은 것을 고르시오.

1

> A _____ did you do last night?
>
> B I helped my mom.

① What   ② Which   ③ Who

④ Whom   ⑤ Whose

2

> A _____ of those two skirts is yours?
>
> B The blue one is mine.

① What   ② Which   ③ Whose

④ Who   ⑤ Why

3 다음 대답의 알맞은 질문을 고르시오.

> She has long, curly hair.

① What do she look?

② What does she look?

③ What does she look like?

④ Which look does she?

⑤ Whose look is this?

4 다음 우리말을 영어로 바르게 옮긴 것을 고르시오.

> Wendy와 Joy 중에 누가 춤에 관심이 있니?

① What is interested in dancing, Wendy and Joy?

② Who are interested in dancing, Wendy and Joy?

③ Who is interested in dancing, Wendy and Joy?

④ Who is interested in dancing, Wendy or Joy?

⑤ Which is interested in dancing, Wendy or Joy?

5 다음 질문의 대답으로 알맞은 것을 고르시오.

> Who gave you this snack?

① Esther was.

② Yes, I was.

③ Rachel did.

④ My friend does.

⑤ No, I didn't give them.

6 빈칸에 들어갈 말이 순서대로 바르게 짝지어진 것을 고르시오.

> • _____ is your nickname?
>
> • _____ won a prize?

① Who - Who   ② Who - What

③ Whose - What   ④ What - Who

⑤ Which - Which

7 다음 질문의 대답으로 알맞은 않은 것을 고르시오.

> What did you do last weekend?

① I arranged my clothes.

② I took a walk in the park.

③ I bought a ring for Mia.

④ I swam in the pool.

⑤ I like planning a trip.

curly 곱슬머리의   look like ~ ~처럼 보이다   snack 간식   nickname 별명   won a prize 상을 타다   arrange 정리하다, 배열하다   plan 계획하다

8 다음 우리말과 같은 뜻이 되도록 주어진 단어를 배열할 때 네 번째로 오는 것을 고르시오.

> William은 무엇을 보고 있니?
>
> (looking, is, William, what, at)

① is   ② at   ③ looking
④ he   ⑤ What

9 빈칸에 공통으로 들어갈 알맞은 것을 고르시오.

> • _____ size do you wear?
> • _____ do you plan to do this weekend?

① What   ② Who   ③ Which
④ Whose   ⑤ How

10 밑줄 친 부분의 쓰임이 나머지와 다른 것을 고르시오.

① What book are you reading?
② What sport do you like?
③ What is your phone number?
④ What color are her eyes?
⑤ What time did you come?

11 다음 중 대화가 어색한 것을 고르시오.

① A Who is that girl?
   B She is my friend.
② A Who is Steve?
   B He is the boy over there.
③ A What do you think of this movie?
   B It is boring.
④ A Which do you like more, salad or soup?
   B I like salad more.
⑤ A What is your favorite movie?
   B I like going to the movies.

12 우리말과 같은 뜻이 되도록 빈칸에 알맞은 의문사를 쓰시오.

> 누가 이 영화의 주인공이니?
>
> = _____ is the main character of this movie?

13 어법상 어색한 부분을 찾아 바르게 고쳐 쓰시오.

> What do you prefer, hot coffee or cold coffee?

_____ → _____

14 빈칸에 알맞은 의문사를 쓰시오.

> 1) _____ grade are you in?
> 2) _____ broke the vase?
> 3) _____ is better, walking or running?

15 주어진 단어를 이용하여 다음 우리말을 영어로 쓰시오.

> 네가 가장 좋아하는 것은 어느 것이니?
>
> (one, is, favorite, your, which)

→ _____

wear 입다, 신다, 쓰다   main character 주인공   grade 학년, 등급

Unit 02 | When, Where, Why, How

① 의문부사

의문부사는 부사의 일종으로, 시간(when), 장소(where), 이유(why), 방법(how)을 물을 때 사용하는 의문사이다.

	When	Where	Why	How
의미	언제	어디에, 어디서	왜	어떻게
쓰임	시간, 날짜, 계절을 물을 때	위치나 장소를 물을 때	이유나 원인을 물을 때	방법, 수단, 상태, 정도를 물을 때
분류	의문부사			
공통점	Yes나 No로 대답하지 않고, 구체적인 내용으로 대답			

② When, Where, Why, How 의문문

be동사가 있는 문장의 의문사 의문문은 『의문사 + be동사 + 주어 ~?』의 형태이고, 일반동사가 있는 문장의 의문사 의문문은 『의문사 + do/does + 주어 + 동사원형 ~?』의 형태이다.

의문사	질문	대답
When	When is your birthday? 너의 생일은 언제니? / When does the play start? 그 연극은 언제 시작하니?	It's May 12. 5월 12일이야. / It starts at 8:10. 그것은 8시 10분에 시작해.
Where	Where are you from? 너는 어디 출신이니? / Where do you live? 너는 어디 사니?	I'm from Korea. 나는 한국 출신이야. / I live in Busan. 나는 부산에 살아.
Why	Why are you late for school? 너는 왜 학교에 지각했니? / Why did you cry yesterday? 너 어제 왜 울었니?	Because the bus was late. 버스가 늦게 왔기 때문이야. / Because I had a headache. 머리가 아팠어.
How	How is it going? 어떻게 지내니? / How does she go to school? 그녀는 어떻게 학교에 가니?	Pretty good. 꽤 잘 지내. / She goes to school by subway. 그녀는 지하철을 타고 학교에 가.

> **Tip**
> 시간을 묻는 when은 what time으로 바꿔 쓸 수 있다.

> **Tip**
> 이유를 묻는 의문사 why가 쓰인 의문문에는 접속사 Because(~때문에)를 이용하여 답할 수 있다.

> **Tip**
> 『How + 형용사/부사 ~?』형태는 '얼마나 ~하니?'의 의미이다.
> How old is he? 그는 몇 살이니?
> How tall is your sister? 너의 여동생은 키가 얼마나 크니?
> How much are these books? 이 책들은 얼마인가요?
> How far is it from here to the park? 여기서 공원까지 얼마나 머니?
> How often do you exercise? 너는 얼마나 자주 운동하니?
> How long will she stay here? 그녀는 여기서 얼마나 머무를 거니?
> How many coats do you have? 너는 얼마나 많은 코트를 갖고 있니?
> How much coffee do you drink? 너는 얼마나 많은 커피를 마시니?

Grammar START

A 다음 괄호 안에서 알맞은 것을 고르시오.

1 A (When / How) do I get there?

  B Go straight and then turn right.

2 A (How / Why) did you invite her?

  B Because she is my best friend.

3 A (Where / When) do you meet her?

  B At the restaurant.

4 A (Why / How) do you feel today?

  B I feel good.

5 A (When / Where) is your guitar lesson?

  B After school.

6 A (How / Why) long is the river?

  B The river has a length of 150 kilometers.

7 A (When / Where) is my umbrella?

  B It's in the closet.

straight 곧바로, 곧장
turn 돌다
invite 초대하다
length 길이
closet 벽장

B 다음 질문에 적절한 대답을 찾아 바르게 연결하시오.

1 How is the weather? •   • ⓐ I bought it at the mall.

2 Why are you so upset? •   • ⓑ Because I lost my wallet.

3 Where did you buy it? •   • ⓒ About 300 meters from here.

4 How old is her daughter? •   • ⓓ She is three years old.

5 How far is the bank from here? •   • ⓔ It's windy and rainy.

6 When do you eat lunch? •   • ⓕ Twelve o'clock.

upset 속상한
daughter 딸
wallet 지갑
windy 바람이 부는
rainy 비가 오는

A 대화를 읽고, 빈칸에 알맞은 의문사를 쓰시오.

1 A _____ did your mom get angry?

   B Because I told a lie.

2 A _____ were you two hours ago?

   B I was in the library.

3 A _____ did you go to the zoo?

   B I went to the zoo by bus.

4 A _____ can I buy some flowers?

   B Just around the corner.

5 A _____ did you read that book?

   B I read it last week.

6 A _____ is your sister's birthday?

   B It is October 12.

get angry 화가 나다
tell a lie 거짓말하다
corner 모퉁이

B 빈칸에 들어갈 알맞은 말을 보기에서 골라 쓰시오. (단, 한 번씩만 쓸 것)

보기 When	How	Where	Why

1 A _____ is the main library?

   B It's next to the church.

2 A _____ many classes does she have a day?

   B She has four classes.

3 A _____ did you go on a picnic?

   B I went on a picnic two weeks ago.

4 A _____ did she go to the subway station?

   B Because she had to see her friend off.

main library 중앙 도서관
go on a picnic 소풍 가다
see off ~을 배웅하다

C 틀린 부분을 찾아 바르게 고쳐 문장을 다시 쓰시오.

begin 시작하다
fire station 소방서
sunglasses 선글라스

1 Where does school begin?

   ➡ _____

2 When are you going now?

   ➡ _____

3 What was the action movie?

   ➡ _____

4 What many hours do you watch TV every day?

   ➡ _____

5 How long is the fire station?

   ➡ _____

6 What are you wearing sunglasses?

   ➡ _____

7 When time did you arrive at the airport?

   ➡ _____

D 우리말과 같은 뜻이 되도록 주어진 단어를 바르게 배열하시오.

relative 친척
move 이사하다

1 너는 언제 너의 친척을 방문했니? (did, your relatives, visit, when, you)

   ➡ _____

2 너는 너의 지갑을 어디서 찾았니? (find, did, where, you, your wallet)

   ➡ _____

3 너는 왜 그렇게 일찍 일어나니? (do, so, you, why, early, get up)

   ➡ _____

4 너는 어디로 이사 가니? (moving, you, to, are, where)

   ➡ _____

1 빈칸에 공통으로 들어갈 알맞은 것을 고르시오.

> • A _____ is the weather outside?
>   B It's warm and sunny.
> • A _____ can I get to the station?
>   B Take bus number 151.

① When   ② Where   ③ How
④ Why   ⑤ What

2 빈칸에 들어갈 알맞은 것을 고르시오.

> A Why are you learning Korean?
> B _____ it is interesting and useful.

① Because   ② If   ③ Before
④ Then   ⑤ Though

3 다음 질문에 대한 대답으로 알맞은 것을 고르시오.

> How long do you brush your teeth?

① Seven.
② Three times a day.
③ For about three minutes.
④ Yes, I am.
⑤ I brush my teeth.

4 다음 우리말을 영어로 바르게 옮긴 것을 고르시오.

> 그녀는 언제 서울에 도착할 수 있니?

① Can she when arrive in Seoul?
② When she can arrive in Seoul?
③ When can she arrives in Seoul?
④ When does she can arrive in Seoul?
⑤ When can she arrive in Seoul?

5 다음 문장을 의문사 Why를 이용한 의문문으로 적절하게 바꾼 것을 고르시오.

> Tom likes writing movie reviews.

① Why Tom likes writing movie reviews?
② Why does Tom like writing movie reviews?
③ Why do Tom likes writing movie reviews?
④ Why do Tom like writing movie reviews?
⑤ Why does Tom likes writing movie reviews?

6 빈칸에 들어갈 말이 나머지와 다른 것을 고르시오.

① _____ long is the bridge?
② _____ can I help you?
③ _____ was she born?
④ _____ do you like your teacher?
⑤ _____ is everything?

7 다음 질문에 대한 대답으로 알맞지 않은 것을 고르시오.

> Where are your sisters?

① I don't know.
② They are in the kitchen.
③ Sorry. I have no idea.
④ Yes, they are at the bus stop.
⑤ They are studying together in my room.

---

review 검토, 논평 bridge 다리, 가교 be born 태어나다 have no idea 전혀 모른다

8 빈칸에 들어갈 알맞은 말을 고르시오.

> A _____ does it take to go to the sports complex?
> B It takes 40 minutes by car.

① Where   ② When   ③ How much
④ How far   ⑤ How long

9 다음 두 문장이 같은 뜻이 되도록 빈칸에 들어갈 알맞은 말을 고르시오.

> What time does the store close?
> = _____ does the store close?

① When   ② How   ③ Where
④ Why   ⑤ Who

[10-11] 다음 중 의문사의 쓰임이 <u>어색한</u> 것을 고르시오.

10 ① Where do you use it?
② Why were your shoes wet?
③ How tall is the basketball player?
④ How many is the perfume?
⑤ When does your class start?

11 ① Where does Olivia live?
② How do you go to school?
③ When does she eat breakfast?
④ When does the next bus arrive?
⑤ Where do you go there?

12 우리말과 같은 뜻이 되도록 빈칸에 알맞은 말을 쓰시오.

> 너는 하루에 얼마나 많이 자니?
> = _____ _____ sleep do you get a day?

13 어법상 <u>어색한</u> 부분을 찾아 바르게 고쳐 쓰시오.

> Where he meets his friend?

_____ → _____

14 주어진 말을 이용하여 다음 질문에 대한 적절한 대답을 완전한 문장으로 쓰시오.

> How often does she buy clothes?
> (twice a month)

→ _____

15 주어진 단어를 이용하여 다음 우리말을 영어로 쓰시오.

> 너는 영화 티켓을 어디서 구하니?
> (movie tickets, get)

→ _____

---

sports complex 스포츠 종합단지   wet 젖은   perfume 향수   live 살다   clothes 옷, 의복   twice 두 번   leave 떠나다

기초 탄탄 2
GRAMMAR

Chapter
6

비교 구문

1 원급 비교

비교급은 문장 안에서 둘 이상의 대상의 성질, 상태, 수량 등을 비교할 때 쓰는 표현이다. 원급 비교는 두 대상이 비슷하거나 같을 때에 『as + 형용사/부사 + as』의 형태로, 같지 않을 때에 『not + as + 형용사/부사 + as』의 형태로 나타낸다.

원급 비교	긍정	부정
의미	~만큼 …한	~만큼 …하지 않은
형태	as + 형용사/부사 + as	not + as + 형용사/부사 + as
예문	This box is as heavy as that one. 이 상자는 저 상자만큼 무겁다.	Jeff is not as strong as Daniel. Jeff는 Daniel만큼 힘이 세지 않다.

2 비교급 비교

두 대상을 비교하여 '~보다 …한'이라는 의미로 형용사나 부사의 기본형에 -er을 붙이거나 more을 붙여 비교급을 만들어 『비교급 + than』의 형태로 나타낸다.

비교급 비교		
의미	~보다 …한	
형태	비교급 + than	more + 원급 + than
예문	Alice is older than Tom. Alice는 Tom보다 나이가 많다.	This book is more expensive than mine. 이 책은 내 것보다 비싸다.

> **Tip**
> 형용사나 부사 앞에 less(~보다 덜 …한)를 붙여 표현할 수 있다.
> This book is less expensive than mine. 이 책은 내 것보다 덜 비싸다.

3 비교급의 변화 규칙

원급	비교급의 변화 규칙	원급과 비교급
대부분의 단어	+ -er	tall → taller, old → older
-e로 끝나는 단어	+ -r	nice → nicer, large → larger
'단모음 + 단자음'으로 끝나는 단어	자음을 한 번 더 쓰고 + -er	big → bigger, hot → hotter
'자음 + y'로 끝나는 단어	y를 i로 바꾸고 + -er	happy → happier, pretty → prettier
-able, -ful, -ous, -less, -ive, -ly 등으로 끝나는 단어 / 2음절 이상의 단어	more + 형용사/부사의 원급	famous → more famous, beautiful → more beautiful
분사(-ing/-ed) 형태로 끝나는 단어	more + 원급	exciting → more exciting
불규칙 변화	–	good, well → better, bad/ill → worse many/much → more, little → less

He is taller than his father.
그는 그의 아버지보다 키가 크다.

The singer is more famous than the movie star.
그 가수는 그 영화 배우보다 유명하다.

> **Tip**
> 비교급 앞에 much, far, even, a lot 등을 써서 '훨씬 더 ~한'의 의미로 비교급을 강조할 수 있다. very, so는 원급을 강조하는 부사로서 비교급을 수식할 수는 없다.
> Today is much colder than yesterday. 오늘은 어제보다 훨씬 더 춥다.
> An elephant is a lot larger than a rabbit. 코끼리는 토끼보다 훨씬 더 크다.

Grammar START

A 다음 형용사의 비교급을 쓰시오.

1 light _____

2 short _____

3 cute _____

4 heavy _____

5 thin _____

6 warm _____

7 quick _____

8 young _____

9 loud _____

10 bright _____

11 wide _____

12 early _____

13 hard _____

14 fast _____

15 cold _____

16 high _____

17 smooth _____

18 difficult _____

19 expensive _____

20 useful _____

light 밝은, 가벼운
cute 귀여운
heavy 무거운
thin 얇은, 마른
quick 빠른
loud 시끄러운
bright 빛나는, 밝은
wide 넓은
fast 빠른
high 높은
smooth 매끈한, 부드러운
difficult 어려운
expensive 비싼
useful 유용한

B 다음 괄호 안에서 알맞은 것을 고르시오.

1 Rabbits are (faster / fastter) than turtles.

2 Spring is (more warm / warmer) than winter.

3 Alice is (younger / youngger) than her sister.

4 This ring is (expensiver / more expensive) than that necklace.

5 Mike's bag is (as / so) light as my bag.

6 My sister drank (littler / less) coffee than yesterday.

7 A watermelon is (more heavier / heavier) than an apple.

8 The movie is as (interesting / more interesting) as this book.

9 The math test was (diffculter / more difficult) than the English test.

turtle 거북이
spring 봄
winter 겨울
ring 반지
expensive 비싼
necklace 목걸이
watermelon 수박
math 수학

A 주어진 단어와 우리말을 이용하여 빈칸에 알맞은 말을 쓰시오.

1 이 과일은 저 사탕만큼 달다. (sweet)

→ This fruit is as _____ as that candy.

2 러시아는 호주보다 춥다. (cold)

→ Russia is _____ than Australia.

3 나는 내 여동생보다 일찍 일어난다. (early)

→ I get up _____ _____ my sister.

4 지리산은 설악산보다 높다. (high)

→ Mt. Jiri is _____ _____ Mt. Seorak.

5 내 담요는 너의 담요만큼 부드럽지 않다. (soft)

→ My blanket is _____ _____ _____ as than yours.

6 이 꽃이 저 꽃보다 아름답다. (beautiful)

→ This flower is _____ _____ than that one.

7 그녀는 그녀의 여동생보다 예쁘다. (pretty)

→ She is _____ _____ her sister.

Mt. (mountain의 약어) 산
blanket 담요

B 두 문장의 의미가 같도록 주어진 단어를 이용하여 빈칸에 알맞은 말을 쓰시오.

1 A taxi is faster than a bus. (slow)

= A bus is _____ _____ a taxi.

2 Today's weather is worse than yesterday's. (good)

= Yesterday's weather is _____ _____ today's.

3 My grandfather is weaker than my father. (strong)

= My father is _____ _____ my grandfather.

4 This desk is larger than that chair. (small)

= That chair is _____ _____ this desk.

weak 약한
strong 강한

C 틀린 부분을 찾아 바르게 고쳐 문장을 다시 쓰시오.

1 An elephant is biger than a hippo.

➡ _____

2 The bathroom is as cleaner as my room.

➡ _____

3 The actress is popular more than the actor.

➡ _____

4 Lily works carefullier than Kelly.

➡ _____

5 Daniel is many taller than John.

➡ _____

6 I like baseball very more than basketball.

➡ _____

7 Pizza is as not delicious as spaghetti.

➡ _____

hippo 하마
carefully
주의 깊게, 정성 들여서
delicious 맛있는

D 우리말과 같은 뜻이 되도록 주어진 단어를 바르게 배열하시오.

1 태양은 달보다 뜨겁다. (the moon, than, the sun, hotter, is)

➡ _____

2 건강은 돈보다 더 중요하다. (is, than, money, more, health, important)

➡ _____

3 달팽이는 치타보다 훨씬 느리다. (cheetahs, than, far, snails, slower, are)

➡ _____

4 내 스마트폰이 저 카메라보다 얇다.
(that, thinner, than, smartphone, my, is, camera)

➡ _____

health 건강
important 중요한
far 훨씬

1 형용사의 원급과 비교급이 바르게 짝지어지지 않은 것을 고르시오.

① nice - nicer

② busy - busyer

③ little - less

④ happy - happier

⑤ interesting - most interesting

2 빈칸에 들어갈 알맞은 것을 고르시오.

> August is _____ than November.

① hot   ② less hot   ③ hotter

④ more hot   ⑤ very hot

3 빈칸에 들어갈 수 없는 것을 고르시오.

> Tom is _____ than Mike.

① funny

② smarter

③ cleverer

④ less friendly

⑤ more handsome

4 빈칸에 들어갈 말이 순서대로 바르게 짝지어진 것을 고르시오.

> • Tim plays sports _____ than me.
>
> • Emma has as _____ books as Jeff does.

① well - many   ② better - more

③ better - many   ④ gooder - more

⑤ gooder - much

5 다음 우리말과 같은 뜻이 되도록 빈칸에 들어갈 알맞은 것을 고르시오.

> 내 피부는 저 아기의 피부보다 건조하다.
>
> = My skin is _____ than the baby's.

① dry   ② drier   ③ dryer

④ dryier   ⑤ more dry

[6-7] 빈칸에 들어갈 수 없는 것을 고르시오.

6
> He is more _____ than me.

① intelligent   ② diligent   ③ thoughtful

④ famous   ⑤ strong

7
> My mom is _____ more beautiful than the actress.

① far   ② even   ③ a lot

④ very   ⑤ much

8 다음 우리말과 같은 뜻이 되도록 주어진 단어를 배열할 때 여섯 번째로 오는 것을 고르시오.

> 이 문제는 저 문제보다 어렵지 않다.
>
> (problem, that, not, is, difficult, this, than, more, one)

① is   ② than   ③ more

④ not   ⑤ difficult

August 8월 November 11월 clever 영리한 handsome 잘생긴 dry 건조한 intelligent 영리한 diligent 성실한, 근면한 thoughtful 사려 깊은

9 표의 내용과 일치하지 <u>않는</u> 문장을 고르시오.

	Sam	Bentley	William
Height (cm)	165	160	170
Weight (km)	55	60	65

① Sam is taller than Bentley.

② Bentley is lighter than William.

③ William is taller than Sam.

④ Bentley is heavier than Sam.

⑤ Sam is shorter than Bentley.

10 밑줄 친 부분 중 어법상 <u>어색한</u> 것을 고르시오.

① China is <u>larger</u> than Korea.

② This doll is <u>prettier</u> than that robot.

③ For me, taste is <u>importanter</u> than price.

④ Gold is <u>more expensive</u> than silver.

⑤ This room is not <u>darker</u> than that one.

11 다음 중 어법상 <u>어색한</u> 문장을 고르시오.

① He is as old as Jina.

② It's colder than yesterday.

③ Cars are safer than motorcycles.

④ You are more good than your picture.

⑤ She is less popular than before.

12 다음 두 문장이 같은 뜻이 되도록 빈칸에 들어갈 알맞은 말을 쓰시오.

> The temperature in the room is lower than the outside temperature.
>
> = The outside temperature is _____ _____ the temperature in the room.

→ _____

13 어법상 <u>어색한</u> 부분을 찾아 바르게 고쳐 쓰시오.

> The milk's taste is badder than the grape juice.

_____ → _____

14 다음 두 문장을 비교급을 이용하여 한 문장으로 바꿔 쓰시오. (긍정문으로)

> • Mary is very careless.
> • Lily is not careless.

→ Mary _____

15 주어진 단어를 바르게 배열하여 다음 우리말을 영어로 쓰시오.

> 롤러코스터는 회전목마보다 훨씬 더 재미있다.
>
> (exciting, a merry-go-round, than, is, more, a rollercoaster, much)

→ _____

_____

gold 금 silver 은 dark 어두운 motorcycle 오토바이 popular 인기 있는 temperature 온도, 기온 careless 부주의한, 조심성 없는
exciting 신나는, 흥미진진한

Unit 02 최상급

1 최상급의 변화 규칙

최상급은 셋 이상을 비교하여 그 중 최고를 말할 때 쓰는 표현이다. 최상급은 형용사나 부사의 원급에 -est를 붙이거나 앞에 most를 붙여서 만들고, '가장 ~한'이라고 해석한다. 최상급 앞에는 the를 붙이는데 동일 대상을 다른 상황과 비교할 때는 붙이지 않는다.

원급	최상급의 변화 규칙	원급과 비교급
대부분의 단어	+ -est	tall → tallest, old → oldest
-e로 끝나는 단어	+ -st	nice → nicest, large → largest
'단모음 + 단자음'으로 끝나는 단어	자음을 한 번 더 쓰고 + -est	big → biggest, hot → hottest
'자음 + y'로 끝나는 단어	y를 i로 바꾸고 + -est	happy → happiest, pretty → prettiest
-able, -ful, -ous, -less, -ive, -ly 등으로 끝나는 단어 / 2음절 이상의 단어	most + 형용사/부사의 원급	famous → most famous, beautiful → most beautiful
분사(-ing/-ed) 형태로 끝나는 단어	most + 원급	exciting → most exciting
불규칙 변화	–	good, well → best, bad/ill → worst many/much → most, little → least

The quiz is the easiest one. 그 퀴즈는 가장 쉬운 것이다.

She is the most popular singer in our country. 그녀는 우리나라에서 가장 인기 있는 가수이다.

The baseball team is the best in the league. 그 야구팀은 리그 내에서 최상위 팀이다.

> **Tip**
>
> 최상급의 비교 범위를 나타낼 때 『in + 단수명사(장소, 집단)』를 쓰거나, 『of + 복수명사/기간 명사』를 써서 범위를 한정할 수 있다.
> The Louvre Museum is the largest museum in the world. 루브르 박물관은 세계에서 가장 큰 박물관이다.
> January is the coldest month of the year. 1월은 일 년 중에 가장 추운 달이다.

2 비교급을 이용한 최상급 표현

원급과 비교급을 이용하여 최상급을 나타낼 수 있다.

최상급	형태	예문
원급을 이용한 최상급 표현	No + 단수명사 + 동사 + as/so + 원급 + as ~ (다른) 어떤 …도 ~만큼 …하지 않다.	This is the most interesting musical. 이것이 가장 재미있는 뮤지컬이다. → No musical is as interesting as this. 다른 어떤 뮤지컬도 이 영화만큼 재미있지 않다.
비교급을 이용한 최상급 표현	비교급 + than any other + 단수명사 다른 어떤 ~보다 더 …한	It is the oldest fossil in the world. 그것은 세계에서 가장 오래된 화석이다. → It is older than any other fossil in the world. 그것은 세계의 다른 어떤 화석보다 더 오래된 것이다.
	No + 단수명사 + 비교급 + than ~ 어떤 무엇/누구도 ~보다 …하지 않은	Korean is the most beautiful language in the world. 한국어는 세계에서 가장 아름다운 언어이다. → No language in the world is more beautiful than Korean. 세계의 어떤 언어도 한국어보다 더 아름답지 않다.

Grammar START

A 다음 형용사의 최상급을 쓰시오.

1 light _____
2 short _____
3 cute _____
4 heavy _____
5 thin _____
6 warm _____
7 quick _____
8 young _____
9 loud _____
10 bright _____

11 wide _____
12 early _____
13 hard _____
14 fast _____
15 cold _____
16 high _____
17 smooth _____
18 difficult _____
19 expensive _____
20 useful _____

B 다음 괄호 안에서 알맞은 것을 고르시오.

1 It is the (longer / longest) river in the world.

2 Kelly is the (tallest / taller) of the three.

3 What is the (fastest / most fast) animal on the Earth?

4 This juice is the (sourest / most sour) in the café.

5 This school is the oldest (building / buildings) in the city.

6 When was the (greater / greatest / most great) moment in your life?

7 Ariana is the (most good / better / best) dancer in the group.

8 She is the (friendliest / most friendly) flight attendant on the airline.

9 These earrings are the (expensivest / most expensive) in the store.

Earth 지구
moment 순간, 잠깐
flight attendant
비행기 승무원
airline 항공사
earring 귀걸이
store 가게, 상점

Grammar **PRACTICE**

A 주어진 단어와 우리말을 이용하여 빈칸에 알맞은 말을 쓰시오.

1 그는 그의 세 형제들 중에서 가장 똑똑하다. (smart)

➡ He is _____ _____ of all three brothers.

2 서울은 한국에서 가장 유명한 도시이다. (famous)

➡ Seoul is _____ _____ _____ city in Korea.

3 바이칼 호수는 지구에서 가장 깊은 호수이다. (deep)

➡ Lake Baikal is _____ _____ lake on the Earth.

4 James는 그의 반에서 가장 무거운 학생이다. (heavy)

➡ James is _____ _____ student in his class.

5 여왕벌은 모든 꿀벌들 중에 가장 크다. (big)

➡ The queen bee is _____ _____ of all the bees.

6 그는 한국에서 가장 인기 있는 가수이다. (popular)

➡ He is _____ _____ _____ singer in Korea.

7 이것은 2018년의 최고의 영화이다. (good)

➡ This is _____ _____ movie of 2018

lake 호수
queen 여왕
bee 꿀벌

B 두 문장의 의미가 같도록 주어진 지시에 맞춰 문장을 완성하시오.

1 This cake is the softest in the bakery. (비교급 이용)

= This cake is _____ in the bakery.

2 This smartphone is the thinnest in the world. (비교급 이용)

= No _____ this smartphone.

3 Russia is the largest country in the world. (원급 이용)

= No _____ Russia.

4 He is the richest person in Korea. (비교급 이용)

= He is _____ in Korea.

bakery 제과점
rich 부유한

C 틀린 부분을 찾아 바르게 고쳐 문장을 다시 쓰시오.

1 I like winter the most in all the seasons.

➡ _____

2 Health is the importantest thing of all.

➡ _____

3 The house is the most attractivest in the town.

➡ _____

4 Tell me the faster way to get to the airport.

➡ _____

5 Time is more precious as any other thing.

➡ _____

6 It was the badest choice of his life.

➡ _____

7 She is most diligent than any other student in her class.

➡ _____

attractive 매력적인
precious 소중한
choice 선택
diligent 근면한, 성실한

D 우리말과 같은 뜻이 되도록 주어진 단어를 바르게 배열하시오.

1 영어 시험이 시험들 중에서 가장 쉬웠다.
(was, of, easiest, all the tests, the English test, the)

➡ _____

2 그것은 내 인생에서 가장 놀라운 경험이었다.
(amazing, was, most, in my life, experience, it, the)

➡ _____

3 이 침대는 이 가게에서 가장 편안하다.
(in the store, the, comfortable, in, this bed, most, is)

➡ _____

amazing 놀라운
experience 경험
comfortable 편안한

1 형용사의 원급과 최상급이 바르게 짝지어지지 <u>않은</u> 것을 고르시오.

① hot - hottest

② early - earliest

③ large - largest

④ heavy - heavyest

⑤ dangerous - most dangerous

2 빈칸에 들어갈 알맞은 것을 고르시오.

The rose is _____ flower in the garden.

① beautiful   ② more beautiful

③ more beautiful than   ④ most beautiful

⑤ the most beautiful

3 밑줄 친 단어를 어법상 올바르게 고친 것을 고르시오.

Science is the <u>useful</u> subject to me.

① useful   ② usefuler

③ most useful   ④ more useful

⑤ most usefuler

4 다음 문장과 의미가 같은 것을 고르시오.

Christina is older than Tony but younger than Aaron.

① Aaron is the youngest of all.

② Tony is the oldest of all.

③ Aaron is the oldest of all.

④ Christina is the youngest of all.

⑤ Christina is the oldest of all.

5 다음 우리말을 영어로 바르게 옮긴 것을 고르시오.

그는 세계에서 가장 빠른 남자이다.

① He is fast man in the world.

② He is faster than the man in the world.

③ He is fastest man in the world.

④ He is the most fast man in the world.

⑤ He is the fastest man in the world.

6 다음 우리말과 같은 뜻이 되도록 빈칸에 들어갈 알맞은 것을 고르시오.

그것은 그의 작품 중에 가장 훌륭한 소설이다.

= It is the _____ novel of all his works.

① good   ② better   ③ most

④ best   ⑤ worst

7 빈칸에 들어갈 famous의 형태가 나머지와 <u>다른</u> 것을 고르시오.

① He is the _____ in the world.

② Baseball is _____ than softball.

③ Which book is the _____ of the three?

④ Let me introduce the _____ place in Seoul.

⑤ How about going to the _____ amusement park in Korea?

introduce 소개하다   place 장소   amusement park 놀이공원

8 다음 우리말과 같은 뜻이 되도록 주어진 단어를 배열할 때 <u>여섯 번째</u>로 오는 것을 고르시오.

> Fred는 그의 세 형제 중에서 가장 공손하다.
>
> (the, brothers, Fred, the, three, most, is, courteous, of)

① of ② the ③ most
④ three ⑤ courteous

9 다음 문장과 의미가 같은 것을 고르시오.

> The strawberries are fresher than any other fruit in the supermarket.

① The strawberries are very fresh.
② Other fruits are fresher than the strawberries.
③ The strawberries are fresher than the apples.
④ No fruit in the supermarket is as fresh as the apples.
⑤ The strawberries are the freshest fruit in the supermarket.

10 밑줄 친 부분이 어법상 <u>틀린</u> 것을 고르시오.

① This was the <u>funniest</u> cartoon of the year.
② Jamie is the <u>cutiest</u> girl in her class.
③ The dictionary is the <u>thickest</u> in the bookcase.
④ Please show me the <u>largest</u> room in the hotel.
⑤ She asked <u>more</u> questions than any other student.

11 다음 중 어법상 <u>어색한</u> 문장을 고르시오.

① It was the most scary movie in my life.
② Peter is the best skater of the three boys.
③ My mom is the most active in my family.
④ He is the slowest boy in his class.
⑤ The movie star was the worst dresser at the festival.

12 다음 두 문장이 같은 뜻이 되도록 빈칸에 들어갈 알맞은 말을 쓰시오.

> Happiness is the most important thing.
>
> = Happiness is _____ _____ _____ any other thing.

→ _____

[13-14] 어법상 <u>어색한</u> 부분을 찾아 바르게 고쳐 쓰시오.

13

> She works the hardest when she is confident.

_____ → _____

14

> It is the weakest dog of the animal hospital.

_____ → _____

15 주어진 단어를 바르게 배열하여 다음 우리말을 영어로 쓰시오.

> 어떤 스포츠도 피겨 스케이팅만큼 아름답지 않다.
>
> (is, no, beautiful, figure skating, sport, more, than)

→ _____
_____

---

courteous 공손한   fresh 신선한   dictionary 사전   bookcase 책장   scary 무서운   active 활동적인, 적극적인   festival 축제   happiness 행복
animal hospital 동물병원

Review TEST 3 ▶ Chapter 5 & Chapter 6

1 다음 중 원급-비교급-최상급이 바르게 짝지어지지 않은 것을 고르시오.

① little - less - least
② early - earlier - earliest
③ big - bigger - biggest
④ famous - famouser - famousest
⑤ careful - more careful - most careful

2 빈칸에 들어갈 알맞은 것을 고르시오.

| A _____ is your dream job? |
| B I want to be a reporter. |

① Who   ② What   ③ How
④ Where   ⑤ When

3 빈칸에 들어갈 말로 적절한 것을 모두 고르시오.

| Apple is _____ in the world. |

① more popular than
② the popularest brand
③ the more popular than
④ the most popular brand
⑤ more popular than any other brand

4 빈칸에 들어갈 말이 순서대로 바르게 짝지어진 것을 고르시오.

| • A _____ is the girl in the red coat? |
| B She is my cousin. |
| • A _____ does the rainy season begin? |
| B It begins in July. |

① What - When   ② What - When
③ Who - When   ④ Who - How
⑤ Where - How

5 빈칸에 들어갈 수 <u>없는</u> 것을 고르시오.

| Jenny walks _____ faster than he. |

① very   ② a lot   ③ much
④ still   ⑤ far

6 주어진 단어를 이용하여 다음 우리말을 영어로 쓰시오. (필요시 어형을 바꿀 것)

| 둘 중 어느 게 더 빠른가요? |
| (one, of the two, fast) |

➡ _____

7 빈칸에 들어갈 말이 순서대로 바르게 짝지어진 것을 고르시오.

| • Susan studied _____ than her sister. |
| • The god Khiron in Greek mythology was the _____. |

① harder - wiser   ② hardest - most wise
③ harder - most wise   ④ hardest - wisest
⑤ harder - wisest

8 다음 우리말을 영어로 바르게 옮긴 것을 고르시오.

| 그 영화는 언제까지 상영되나요? |

① How far will the movie run?
② How long will the movie run?
③ How tall will the movie run?
④ How often will the movie run?
⑤ How many will the movie run?

9 빈칸에 들어갈 말이 순서대로 바르게 짝지어진 것을 고르시오.

> William과 Brad 중에서 누가 더 힘이 세니?
>
> ➡ _____ is _____, William or Brad?

① Who - stronger   ② Who - strongest

③ What - stronger   ④ What - strong

⑤ What - strongest

10 다음 우리말을 영어로 바르게 옮긴 것을 고르시오.

> 너는 록 음악과 재즈 음악 중에서 어느 음악을 더 좋아하니?

① Do you like rock or jazz music?

② Why do you like rock or jazz music?

③ What music do you like better, rock or jazz?

④ Which music do you like better, rock or jazz?

⑤ How do you like better, rock or jazz music?

11 다음 중 어법상 올바른 문장을 고르시오.

① When does the train comes?

② What do your father do on weekends?

③ Where do he practices the piano?

④ Which class does your sister chose?

⑤ Why does your mom drink milk every day?

12 주어진 단어를 바르게 배열하여 다음 우리말을 영어로 쓰시오.

> 너는 여행에서 얼마나 많은 돈을 썼니?
>
> (did, how, much, spend, on the trip, you, money)

➡ _____

   _____

13 다음 짝지어진 두 문장의 의미가 <u>다른</u> 것을 고르시오.

① What time do you leave?

   = When do you leave?

② Amy speaks Chinese better than Lynn.

   = Lynn speaks Chinese worse than Amy.

③ This park is even cleaner than that one.

   = This park is so cleaner than that one.

④ He is the greatest player on the team.

   = No player on the team is greater than him.

⑤ The coffee is cheaper than the ice cream.

   = The ice cream is more expensive than the coffee.

[14-15] 다음은 Mary와 Wendy의 이번 중간고사의 시험 성적이다. 빈칸에 알맞은 말을 쓰시오.

Mary		Wendy	
Subject	Score	Subject	Score
English	100	English	100
Korean	90	Korean	80
Math	80	Math	90

14 주어진 단어를 이용하여 Mary와 Wendy의 국어 점수를 비교하는 문장을 완성하시오.

> In Korean, Mary got a _____ _____
>
> _____ _____.
>
> (high, score)

➡ _____

15 최상급을 이용해 다음 문장을 완성하시오.

> They got their _____ _____ in English.

➡ _____

Chapter
7

명령문과 감탄문

Unit 01 | 명령문

1 명령문

명령문은 '~해라' 또는 '~하지 마라' 등의 명령, 금지, 요청의 의미를 나타내는 문장이다.

2 긍정 명령문과 부정 명령문

의미에 따라 긍정 명령문과 부정 명령문으로 나눌 수 있으며, 주어(you)를 생략하고 동사원형으로 시작한다.
부정 명령문은 Don't로 시작한다.

명령문	긍정 명령문	부정 명령문
의미	~해라	~하지 마라
형태	동사원형	Don't + 동사원형
예문	Open the window. 창문을 열어라. Be quiet. 조용히 해라.	Don't close the window. 창문을 닫지 마라. Don't be afraid. 두려워하지 마라.
유사형	강한 의무 나타내는 조동사 must (~해야 한다)	강한 금지 나타내는 조동사 must not (~하면 안 된다)

TIP
보다 강한 금지를 나타낼 때에는 『Never + 동사원형』의 형태로 쓸 수 있다.

TIP
명령문의 앞이나 뒤에 please를 붙이면 좀 더 정중한 부탁이나 요청의 의미를 나타낼 수 있다.
문장 끝에 please를 붙일 때에는 보통 please 앞에 콤마(,)를 붙인다.
Please open the window. 창문 좀 열어주세요.
= Open the window, please.

3 명령문, and/or

명령문 뒤에 and 또는 or을 붙이면 다음과 같은 의미를 나타낼 수 있다.

형태	예문
명령문, and (~해라, 그러면 …할 것이다)	Study hard, and you'll get a good grade. 열심히 공부해라, 그러면 너는 좋은 성적을 받을 것이다.
명령문, or (~해라, 그렇지 않으면 …할 것이다)	Hurry up, or you'll miss the bus. 서둘러라, 그렇지 않으면 너는 버스를 놓칠 것이다.

TIP
『Let's + 동사원형』의 형태는 '~하자'라는 의미의 권유 명령문이다.
『Let's not + 동사원형』은 '~하지 말자'라고 해석한다.
Let's play basketball. 농구하자.
Let's not open the window. 창문을 열지 말자.

Grammar **START**

A 다음 괄호 안에서 알맞은 것을 고르시오.

1 (Watch / Watches) out for cars.

2 (Don't / Doesn't) be late for school.

3 (Not / Never) say that again.

4 (Are / Be) nice to your friends.

5 (Clean / Cleans) your room.

6 (Be / Are) careful with the knife.

7 Don't (is / be) silly.

8 Don't (make / making) any noise.

9 Please (pass / passing) me the scissors.

10 (Isn't / Don't) run in the restaurant.

late 늦은
careful 조심하는
knife 칼, 나이프
silly 어리석은
make a noise
시끄럽게 하다
pass 건네주다

B 다음 문장을 읽고, 명령문 뒤에 and와 or 중 알맞은 것을 쓰시오.

1 Be careful, _____ you may get hurt.

2 Ask questions, _____ you will learn a lot.

3 Don't tell lies, _____ everybody will dislike you.

4 Walk fast, _____ you can't arrive in time.

5 Be quiet, _____ your baby sister can stay asleep.

6 Start now, _____ you will be able to finish quickly.

7 Do the dishes, _____ your mom will get mad.

8 Be honest, _____ you will get her trust.

get hurt 다치다
learn 배우다
dislike 싫어하다
arrive 도착하다
in time 제 시간에
quickly 빨리
get mad 화가 나다
trust 신뢰

Grammar **PRACTICE**

A   주어진 단어와 우리말을 이용하여 빈칸에 알맞은 말을 쓰시오.

1   지금 이를 닦아라. (brush)

➡ _____ your teeth now.

2   여기서 사진을 찍지 마시오. (take)

➡ _____ _____ pictures here.

3   조금 더 크게 말씀해 주세요. (speak)

➡ _____ more loudly, _____.

4   교실에서 뛰지 말아라. (run)

➡ _____ _____ in the classroom.

5   불을 꺼라, 그러면 우리는 에너지를 절약할 수 있다. (turn)

➡ _____ off the light, _____ we can save energy.

6   약속을 어기지 말아라. (break)

➡ _____ _____ your promises.

7   정원에 물을 주세요. (water)

➡ _____ the garden, please.

8   컴퓨터 게임을 너무 많이 하지 말아라. (play)

➡ _____ _____ computer games too much.

9   쓰레기를 버려라. (throw)

➡ _____ away the trash.

10   물을 좀 마시자. (drink)

➡ _____ _____ some water.

11   영어 수업 시간에는 한국어로 말하지 말아라. (speak)

➡ _____ _____ Korean in English class.

12   다시는 그러지 말아라, 그렇지 않으면 너는 어려움에 처할 것이다. (do)

➡ _____ _____ that again, _____ you'll be in trouble.

brush 솔질하다
loudly 큰 소리로
turn off 끄다
save 절약하다
water 물을 주다
break 깨다
promise 약속
trash 쓰레기
throw 던지다
throw away 버리다
trouble 문제, 곤란

B 다음 문장을 긍정 명령문 또는 부정 명령문으로 바꿔 쓰시오.

boil 끓이다
pot 냄비
rude 무례한
in class 수업중

1 You are kind to others.

[긍정] ➡ _____

2 You are on time.

[긍정] ➡ _____

3 You boil water in a pot.

[긍정] ➡ _____

4 You do your homework.

[긍정] ➡ _____

5 You are rude to your parents.

[부정] ➡ _____

6 You eat too much chocolate.

[부정] ➡ _____

7 You draw on the wall.

[부정] ➡ _____

8 You use your cellphone in class.

[부정] ➡ _____

C 주어진 말을 이용하여 다음 우리말을 영어로 쓰시오.

waste 낭비하다

1 너의 시간을 낭비하지 말아라. (waste)

➡ _____

2 서두르지 말자. (hurry)

➡ _____

3 일찍 잠자리에 들어라. (early)

➡ _____

4 조용히 해라, 그렇지 않으면 그 아기가 깰 것이다. (quiet, wake up)

➡ _____

1 빈칸에 들어갈 알맞은 것을 고르시오.

> _____ an umbrella. It may rain.

① Take   ② Taking   ③ Be take

④ Takes   ⑤ To take

2 다음 두 문장이 같은 뜻이 되도록 빈칸에 들어갈 알맞은 말을 고르시오.

> Wash your hands first.
>
> = You _____ wash your hands first.

① will   ② can   ③ must

④ would   ⑤ are able to

3 다음 문장을 명령문으로 올바르게 바꾼 것을 고르시오.

> You are patient all the time.

① Patient all the time.

② Are patient all the time.

③ Do patient all the time.

④ You be patient all the time.

⑤ Be patient all the time.

4 빈칸에 들어갈 알맞은 것을 모두 고르시오.

> Many people are waiting in line here.
> _____ cut in line.

① Be   ② Not   ③ Don't

④ Aren't   ⑤ Never

5 다음 우리말과 같은 뜻이 되도록 빈칸에 알맞은 것을 고르시오.

> 나한테 화내지 마.
>
> = Don't _____ angry with me.

① is   ② are   ③ do

④ you   ⑤ be

6 빈칸에 들어갈 알맞은 것을 고르시오.

> Practice the piano, _____ you can play it very well.

① or   ② and   ③ but

④ so   ⑤ because

7 다음에 이어서 나올 수 있는 가장 자연스러운 문장을 고르시오.

> It's very cold outside.

① Do the dishes.

② Wear a coat.

③ Drink some water.

④ Take off your shoes.

⑤ Turn on the air conditioner.

---

first 먼저, 우선 patient 인내심 있는 all the time 항상, 줄곧 cut in line 새치기 하다

8 다음 문장과 바꿔 쓸 수 있는 것을 고르시오.

> Don't put on a hat indoors.

① Please put on a hat indoors.
② You won't put on a hat indoors.
③ Never put on a hat indoors.
④ You have to put on a hat indoors.
⑤ You don't like to put on a hat indoors.

9 다음 우리말을 영어로 바르게 옮긴 것을 고르시오.

> 네 남동생과 싸우지 마라.

① Fight with your brother.
② Not fight with your brother.
③ Doesn't fight with your brother.
④ Never fighting with your brother.
⑤ Don't fight with your brother.

10 다음 중 도서관에서 지켜야 할 규칙으로 적절하지 <u>않은</u> 것을 고르시오.

① Don't run.
② Don't speak loudly.
③ Don't eat any food.
④ Answer the phone outside.
⑤ Don't put the books back.

11 다음 중 어법상 <u>어색한</u> 문장을 고르시오.

① Don't be shy.
② Never drive fast.
③ Don't be do that.
④ Get some rest.
⑤ Please tell me the secret.

12 빈칸에 공통으로 들어갈 알맞은 말을 쓰시오.

> • Don't _____ mad about her lie.
> • Boys and girls, _____ ambitious.

13 다음 두 문장이 같은 뜻이 되도록 빈칸에 알맞은 말을 쓰시오.

> Don't forget our appointment.
> = _____ forget our appointment.

14 다음 문장을 부정문으로 바꿔 쓰시오.

> Set the alarm for seven o'clock.

→ _____

15 주어진 단어를 바르게 배열하여 다음 우리말을 영어로 쓰시오.

> 대화 도중에 휴대폰을 보지 말아라.
> (your cellphone, the conversation, don't, during, look at)

→ _____

---

put on ~을 입다/쓰다   indoor 실내에서   answer the phone 전화를 받다   put back ~을 제자리에 갖다 두다   get a rest 쉬다   mad 화를 내는
ambitious 야심 있는   appointment 약속   set 맞추다, 설정하다   during ~중에

① 감탄문

감탄문은 기쁨, 슬픔, 놀람 등을 나타내는 표현으로 '정말 ~하구나!'라고 해석한다. 감탄문은 『What + a/an + 형용사 + 명사 + 주어 + 동사!』 또는 『How + 형용사/부사 + 주어 + 동사!』의 형태이며 뒤에 오는 '주어 + 동사'는 생략할 수 있다.

② What 감탄문과 How 감탄문

What으로 시작하는 감탄문은 『What + a/an + 형용사 + 명사 + 주어 + 동사!』의 형태이며, How로 시작하는 감탄문은 『How + 형용사/부사 + 주어 + 동사!』의 형태이다.

감탄문	What으로 시작하는 감탄문	How로 시작하는 감탄문
의미	정말 ~하구나!	
형태	What + a/an + 형용사 + 명사 + (주어 + 동사)!	How + 형용사/부사 + (주어 + 동사)!
예문	What a nice car! 멋진 차구나! What a great student you are! 너는 정말 훌륭한 학생이구나! What a beautiful flower it is! 정말 아름다운 꽃이구나! What a big balloon you have! 너는 정말 큰 풍선을 가지고 있구나!	How pretty you are! 너는 정말 귀엽구나! How exciting the game is! 그 경기는 정말 신나는구나! How fast she runs! 그녀는 정말 빨리 달리는구나! How wonderfully they sing! 그들은 정말 멋지게 노래 부르는구나!

Tip

what으로 시작하는 감탄문에서도 명사가 복수이거나 셀 수 없는 명사일 경우에는 a(n)을 쓰지 않는다.
What interesting books! 정말 재미있는 책들이구나!
What beautiful sunshine! 정말 아름다운 햇살이구나!

③ How로 시작하는 감탄문과 의문문의 비교

How로 시작하는 감탄문은 『How + 형용사/부사 + 주어 + 동사!』의 어순이며,
How로 시작하는 의문문은 『How + 형용사/부사 + 동사 + 주어?』의 어순으로 주어와 동사의 위치가 다르다.

· 감탄문: How tall he is! 그는 정말 키가 크구나!
· 의문문: How tall is he? 그는 키가 몇이니?

A 다음 괄호 안에서 알맞은 것을 고르시오.

1 (What / How) a creative idea!

2 (What / How) wonderful the festival is!

3 (What / How) a nice cap!

4 (What / How) cheap the shirt is!

5 How pretty (the girl is / is the girl)!

6 (What / How) tall the tree is!

7 (What / How) an amazing story it is!

8 (What / How) nice weather!

9 (What / How) smart your brother is!

10 What a kind boy (he is / they are)!

creative 창의적인
festival 축제
cheap 싼
cap 모자
shirt 셔츠
amazing 놀라운
weather 날씨

B 빈칸에 What 또는 How를 넣어 감탄문을 완성하시오.

1 _____ active he is!

2 _____ cute babies they are!

3 _____ beautiful eyes she has!

4 _____ boring the movie is!

5 _____ delicious this pizza is!

6 _____ a great work her painting is!

7 _____ a big dog you have!

8 _____ a large room it is!

active 적극적인, 활동적인
work 작품
boring 지루한

Grammar **PRACTICE**

A 다음 문장을 감탄문으로 바꿀 때, 빈칸에 알맞은 말을 쓰시오.

1 It is a very touching movie.

➡ What _____ it is!

2 She is a very famous movie star.

➡ What _____ she is!

3 This story is very funny.

➡ How _____ this story is!

4 The old lady is very rich.

➡ How _____ the old lady is!

5 They have really various hobbies.

➡ What _____ they have!

6 The kangaroo jumps really high.

➡ How _____ the kangaroo jumps!

touching 감동적인
rich 부유한
various 다양한
hobby 취미

B 주어진 말을 이용하여 감탄문을 완성하시오.

1 그는 정말 힘이 센 남자구나! (strong)

➡ _____ he is!

2 그것은 정말 신선한 과일이구나! (fresh)

➡ _____ it is!

3 그것은 매우 밝은 달이구나! (bright)

➡ _____ it is!

4 그 책상은 정말 낮구나! (low)

➡ _____ the desk is!

5 공기가 매우 건조하구나! (dry)

➡ _____ the air is!

strong 튼튼한, 힘센
fresh 신선한
bright 밝은
low 낮은
dry 건조한

C 주어진 문장을 What 또는 How로 시작하는 감탄문으로 바꾸어 쓰시오.

1 The room is very clean.

   ➡ _____

2 You have a really big mirror.

   ➡ _____

3 This is a very slow computer.

   ➡ _____

4 I am very happy.

   ➡ _____

5 It is a really small world.

   ➡ _____

6 The music is very loud.

   ➡ _____

7 The candy has a really sour flavor.

   ➡ _____

mirror 거울
sour 맛이 신
flavor 맛, 향

D 우리말과 같은 뜻이 되도록 주어진 단어를 바르게 배열하시오.

1 날씨 참 좋다! (day, what, a, beautiful)

   ➡ _____

2 그 아기가 얼마나 사랑스러운지! (lovely, how, is, the baby)

   ➡ _____

3 그 코트는 정말 두껍구나! (the coat, thick, how, is)

   ➡ _____

4 그것은 정말 멋있는 신발이다! (nice, they, what, shoes, are)

   ➡ _____

lovely 사랑스러운
thick 두꺼운

1 다음 문장을 감탄문으로 바꿀 때, 빈칸에 들어갈 알맞은 것을 고르시오.

> This dress is very pretty.
>
> → _____ this dress is!

① How ② What ③ What pretty
④ How pretty ⑤ How very pretty

2 빈칸에 들어갈 말이 순서대로 바르게 짝지어진 것을 고르시오.

> • _____ terrific!
>
> • _____ a tall building!

① What - What ② What - How ③ How - What
④ How - Why ⑤ How - How

3 다음 문장에서 생략할 수 있는 부분을 고르시오.

> How colorful the flowers are!

① How ② are ③ the flowers
④ colorful ⑤ the flowers are

4 밑줄 친 우리말을 영어로 옮긴 문장이 <u>어색한</u> 것을 고르시오.

> A <u>정말 멋진 파티야!</u>
>
> B I agree with you.

① How nice the party is!
② What a nice party!
③ What nice the party is!
④ It's a really nice party.
⑤ What a nice party it is!

5 다음 문장과 의미가 같은 것을 고르시오.

> What an expensive air conditioner!

① Is the air conditioner expensive?
② It's quite a cheap air conditioner.
③ It's not an expensive air conditioner.
④ How expensive the air conditioner is!
⑤ What do you think about the air conditioner?

6 다음 우리말을 영어로 옮긴 문장이 <u>어색한</u> 것을 고르시오.

> 정말 귀여운 토끼구나!

① What a cute rabbit!
② How a rabbit cute it is!
③ How cute the rabbit is!
④ What a cute rabbit it is!
⑤ The rabbit is very cute.

7 빈칸에 들어갈 말이 나머지와 <u>다른</u> 것을 고르시오.

① _____ cold it is!
② _____ a nice gift!
③ _____ well she dances!
④ _____ small the dog is!
⑤ _____ beautiful this ring is!

---

terrific 멋진, 훌륭한 colorful 형형색색의, 다채로운 agree 동의하다 air conditioner 에어컨

8 다음 중 감탄문으로 바꾼 문장이 올바르지 <u>않은</u> 것을 고르시오.

① It is a very nice car.

→ What a nice car!

② Jennifer cooks very well.

→ How well Jennifer cooks!

③ They are very good singers.

→ What good singers they are!

④ She is a very cute girl.

→ How cute she is!

⑤ He speaks very quietly.

→ How quietly he speaks!

9 다음 중 감탄문으로 올바르게 바꾼 것을 고르시오.

① You are very handsome.

→ How handsome you are!

② This is a really wonderful gift.

→ What wonderful gift this is!

③ These are very nice pants.

→ What a nice pants these are!

④ Your dog is very clever.

→ What clever is your dog!

⑤ It's a very cloudy day.

→ What cloudy day it is!

10 다음 중 어법상 올바른 문장을 고르시오.

① What tall she is!

② What a lovely day!

③ How fast boy he runs!

④ What delicious orange it is!

⑤ What good a computer it is!

11 다음 중 어법상 어색한 문장을 고르시오.

① How far is it!　　② What a long line!

③ How busy you are!　　④ What spicy noodles!

⑤ What a wonderful color!

12 다음 빈칸에 공통으로 들어갈 알맞은 말을 쓰시오.

- _____ a good teacher he is!

- _____ is he wearing on his head?

13 다음 두 문장이 같은 뜻이 되도록 빈칸에 들어갈 알맞은 말을 쓰시오.

Your brother is very smart.

= _____ _____ your brother is!

→ _____

14 다음 문장이 모두 같은 뜻이 되도록 빈칸에 들어갈 알맞은 말을 쓰시오.

She is a really fantastic singer.

= What a _____ _____ she is!

= How fantastic she is!

→ _____

15 주어진 단어를 바르게 배열하여 다음 우리말을 영어로 쓰시오.

그것은 최악의 경기구나!

(it, a, what, is, game, terrible)

→ _____

---

quietly 조용하게　handsome 잘생긴　clever 영리한, 똑똑한　spicy 매운　noodle 국수　fantastic 환상적인　terrible 끔찍한, 형편없는

기초 탄탄 2
GRAMMAR

전치사

1 **전치사**

전치사는 명사, 대명사 앞에 놓여 시간, 장소, 수단, 목적 등을 나타낸다. 대표적으로 시간과 장소를 나타내는 전치사가 있다.

2 **시간의 전치사**

전치사	뜻	쓰임	예문
at	~에	+ 구체적인 시각 및 시점	The class will start at 2 o'clock. 그 수업은 2시에 시작할 것이다.
on		+ 특정한 날짜나 요일	Amy will return home on Tuesday. Amy는 화요일에 집으로 돌아올 것이다.
in		+ 년, 월, 계절 등 긴 시간	My family moved to Seoul in May. 우리 가족은 5월에 서울로 이사했다.
by	~까지	일회성 동작, 상태의 완료	He has to finish the work by 6 o'clock. 그는 6시까지 그 일을 마쳐야 한다.
until		지속적 동작, 상태의 완료	I will watch TV until 3 o'clock. 나는 3시까지 TV를 볼 것이다.
before	~ 전에	과거와 미래 시제 모두와 쓰임	Don't answer the phone before 3 o'clock. 3시 전에 전화를 받지 말아라.
after	~ 후에		We went to the movie after 7 o'clock. 우리는 7시 이후에 영화를 보러 갔다.
for	~ 동안	+ 숫자가 포함된 구체적 기간	He has to stay in the hospital for three months. 그는 3개월 동안 병원에 있어야 한다.
during		+ 특정 기간	I met many of my friends during summer vacation. 나는 여름 방학 동안에 많은 친구들을 만났다.

> **Tip**
>
> 미래 시제와 사용되는 시간 전치사 in은 '(지금부터) ~후에'라는 뜻으로 시간의 경과를 나타내기도 한다.
> Mike will arrive in two hours. Mike는 2시간 후에 도착할 것이다.

3 **장소의 전치사**

전치사	뜻	쓰임	예문
at	~에	+ 구체적인 지점 등 좁은 장소	Patrick is waiting for me at the bus stop. Patrick은 버스 정류장에서 나를 기다리고 있다.
in	~(안)에	+ 공간 내부나 도시, 국가, 하늘 등 넓은 장소	There are two parrots in the cage. 새장 안에 두 마리의 앵무새가 있다.
on	~ 위에	표면에 접촉해 있는 것	I found some coins on the floor. 나는 바닥에서 동전을 약간의 동전을 발견했다.
over		표면 위에 떨어져 있는 것	The birds are flying over the tree. 그 새들이 나무 위를 날고 있다.
under	~ 아래에	표면 아래에 떨어져 있는 것	There is a cat under the tree. 나무 아래에 고양이 한 마리가 있다.
next to, by, beside	~ 옆에	다양하게 쓰임	I left my glasses next to the book. 나는 책 옆에 내 안경을 두었다.
in front of	~ 앞에		Nancy is sitting in front of Peter. Nancy는 Peter 앞에 앉아 있다.
behind	~ 뒤에		The bakery is behind the hospital. 그 제과점은 병원 뒤에 있다.

> **Tip**
>
> 기타 주요 전치사
> for ~때문에
> by (+ 교통수단)
> ~을 타고
> with ~을 가지고, ~와
> about ~에 대해
> except ~을 제외하고
> against ~에 반대하여
> between (둘)
> ~ 사이에
> among (셋 이상)
> ~ 사이에

Grammar **START**

A 다음 문장에서 알맞은 전치사를 고르시오.

1 (In / On / At) the morning, it was sunny.

2 What will you do (at / in / on) the weekend?

3 She seldom has coffee (at / in / on) night.

4 I usually have breakfast (in / on / at) 8 o'clock.

5 Jeff went to Texas (in / on / at) April 9.

6 I always go to sleep (in / before / on) midnight.

7 All of the students have to stay at school (by / until / for) 4:30.

8 Einstein made important discoveries (at / on / in) the 20th century.

9 They played the piano (during / for) music class.

seldom 거의 ~ 않는
midnight 자정, 밤 12시
go to sleep 잠들다
stay 계속 있다, 머무르다
discovery 발견

B 다음 문장에서 알맞은 말을 보기에서 골라 쓰시오. (단, 한 번씩만 쓸 것)

보기	at	on	in	under

1 Noah는 나무 아래에서 쉬고 있다.

➡ Noah is resting _____ a tree.

2 서점은 1층에 있다.

➡ A bookstore is _____ the first floor.

3 Ann은 열쇠를 집에 두고 왔다.

➡ Ann left her key _____ home.

4 하늘에 있는 북극성은 아름다워 보인다.

➡ The North Star _____ the sky looks beautiful.

rest 쉬다
bookstore 서점
key 열쇠
leave 두고 오다
the North Star 북극성

A 다음 문장에서 알맞은 전치사를 보기에서 골라 쓰시오.

보기	in	at	for	by	with	about	on	under

wall 댐, 벽
plane 비행기
river 강
flow 흐른다
bridge 다리
cave 동굴

1 There is a picture _____ the wall.

2 Thank you _____ your help.

3 We will go to L.A. _____ plane.

4 Daniel knows _____ the accident.

5 The river flows _____ the bridge.

6 It is the longest cave _____ the world.

7 A big concert took place _____ the concert hall.

8 I had a great time _____ my family.

B 주어진 단어와 우리말을 이용하여 빈칸에 알맞은 말을 쓰시오.

1 나는 방학 동안에 책 세 권을 읽었다. (my vacation)

➡ I read three books _____.

flute 플루트

2 Cathy는 매일 2시간씩 플루트를 연주한다. (two hours)

➡ Cathy plays the flute _____ every day.

3 나는 저녁식사 후에 Steve를 만날 것이다. (dinner)

➡ I will meet him _____.

4 그 도서관은 월요일마다 문을 닫는다. (Mondays)

➡ The library closes _____.

5 12월에는 날씨가 어떠니? (December)

➡ What is the weather like _____?

C 밑줄 친 부분을 바르게 고쳐 문장을 다시 쓰시오.

1 It takes five hours <u>on</u> train.

➡ _____

2 Mia met Harry <u>in</u> the airport.

➡ _____

3 He did his homework <u>in front of</u> dinner.

➡ _____

4 She will make a cake <u>at</u> his birthday.

➡ _____

5 Don't touch it <u>in</u> your hands.

➡ _____

6 My brother gets up late <u>on</u> the morning.

➡ _____

7 There was a soccer game <u>among</u> Korea and Japan yesterday.

➡ _____

train 기차
airport 공항

D 우리말과 같은 뜻이 되도록 주어진 단어를 바르게 배열하시오.

1 나는 창문 옆에 앉아 있었다. (was, by, the window, sitting, I)

➡ _____

2 영화가 상영되는 동안에 내 휴대폰 벨이 울렸다. (rang, the movie, during, my cellphone)

➡ _____

3 그들은 3개월 동안 그 프로젝트를 수행했다. (three months, did, they, the project, for)

➡ _____

4 나는 군중들 속에서 익숙한 얼굴을 봤다. (familiar, I, a, the crowd, saw, face, in)

➡ _____

ring 울리다
familiar 익숙한, 친숙한
crowd 군중, 사람들

1 빈칸에 들어갈 알맞은 것을 고르시오.

> The Winter Olympics are usually held
> _____ February.

① in   ② on   ③ at
④ for   ⑤ over

2 빈칸에 들어갈 말이 순서대로 바르게 짝지어진 것을 고르시오.

> • She gave her mom a carnation _____
>   Parents' Day.
> • Mike is studying _____ the library.

① on - over   ② in - in
③ at - on   ④ in - on
⑤ on - in

3 빈칸에 들어갈 말이 나머지와 <u>다른</u> 것을 고르시오 .

① The music show is _____ May 20.
② Mary has four classes _____ Monday.
③ He woke up _____ 9:30 last Sunday.
④ They exchanged presents _____ Christmas.
⑤ My family went to the zoo _____ my birthday.

4 밑줄 친 부분과 바꿔 쓸 수 있는 것을 고르시오.

> The hospital is <u>next to</u> the bank.

① in   ② over   ③ under
④ beside   ⑤ in front of

5 다음 우리말을 영어로 바르게 옮긴 것을 고르시오.

> 공연 중에 사진을 찍으시면 안 됩니다.

① You must not take pictures at the performance.
② You must not take pictures for the performance.
③ You must not take pictures during the performance.
④ You must not take pictures on the performance.
⑤ You must not take pictures in the performance.

6 빈칸에 들어갈 알맞은 것을 고르시오.

> A Did you hear _____ the school festival?
> B No, I didn't.

① about   ② by   ③ with
④ against   ⑤ for

7 밑줄 친 부분의 쓰임이 나머지와 <u>다른</u> 것을 고르시오.

① The baby sleeps <u>on</u> the bed.
② There are cats <u>under</u> the desk.
③ We will go skiing <u>in</u> winter.
④ I met him <u>at</u> the subway station.
⑤ A tree is <u>in front of</u> my house.

---

the Winter Olympics 동계 올림픽   Parents' Day 어버이날   exchange 교환하다   present 선물   performance 공연   take a picture 사진을 찍다
subway station 지하철역

8 다음 두 문장이 같은 뜻이 되도록 빈칸에 들어갈 알맞은 말을 고르시오.

> Cathy washed her face before breakfast.
>
> = Cathy had breakfast _____ washing her face.

① for   ② after   ③ between
④ about   ⑤ during

9 빈칸에 들어갈 말이 나머지와 <u>다른</u> 것을 고르시오.

① Mix the flour _____ the water.
② Amy met many foreigners _____ the trip.
③ The girl rubbed her eyes _____ her hands.
④ He is breaking the ice _____ a hammer.
⑤ I visited my grandmother's house _____ my aunt.

10 다음 중 어법상 <u>어색한</u> 것을 고르시오.

> Brian ① is going ② to listen ③ to music ④ on 11 o'clock ⑤ in the morning.

11 밑줄 친 부분의 쓰임이 <u>잘못된</u> 것을 고르시오.

① She paid <u>by</u> cash.
② My father works <u>in</u> London.
③ The boys are talking <u>about</u> baseball.
④ I dropped the ball <u>on</u> the ground.
⑤ Many cars are driving <u>over</u> the bridge.

12 빈칸에 공통으로 들어갈 알맞은 말을 쓰시오.

> • My summer vacation starts _____ July 20.
> • There are two books _____ the bench.

13 다음 두 문장이 같은 뜻이 되도록 빈칸에 들어갈 알맞은 말을 쓰시오.

> The bed is behind the table.
>
> = The table is _____ _____ _____ the bed.

→ _____

14 어법상 <u>어색한</u> 부분을 찾아 바르게 고쳐 쓰시오.

> I graduated from elementary school at 2018.

_____ → _____

15 주어진 단어를 바르게 배열하여 다음 우리말을 영어로 쓰시오.

> 저 일곱 명 중에서 네가 아는 소년은 얼마나 많니?
>
> (do, how many, those seven, know, you, among, boys)

→ _____

_____

---

foreigner 외국인   trip 여행   hammer 망치   rub 문지르다, 비비다   cash 현금   pay 지불하다   drop 떨어뜨리다   graduate 졸업하다

1 등위접속사

접속사는 단어와 단어, 구와 구, 문장과 문장을 서로 연결해주는 말이다. 그것을 대등하게 연결해 주는 말을 등위접속사라고 한다.

등위접속사	예문
and (그리고)	I bought fruits and vegetables at the supermarket. 나는 슈퍼마켓에서 과일과 야채를 샀다.
or (또는)	Will you play soccer or go to the movies? 너 축구 할래, 아니면 영화 볼래?
but (그러나, 하지만)	The necklace is pretty but expensive. 그 목걸이는 예쁘지만 비싸다.
so (그래서)	She was sad, so she cried. 그녀는 슬펐다, 그래서 울었다.

2 종속접속사

종속접속사는 종속절을 주절에 연결할 때 쓰는 말로 시간, 이유, 조건 등을 나타낸다.

종속접속사		예문
시간의 부사절을 이끄는 접속사	when (~할 때)	When I was a boy, I enjoyed fishing. 내가 소년이었을 때, 나는 낚시하는 것을 즐겼다.
	while (~ 동안)	While I was studying, it began to rain. 내가 공부하는 동안, 비가 내리기 시작했다.
	before (~ 전에)	Before I took a walk, I had dinner. 나는 산책하기 전에, 저녁을 먹었다.
	after (~ 후에)	After the train left, he arrived. 기차가 떠난 후에, 그가 도착했다.
	until (~할 때까지)	Please wait for me until the meeting is over. 회의가 끝날 때까지 나를 기다려 주세요.
이유의 부사절을 이끄는 접속사	because (~ 때문에)	I can't buy it because I have no money. 나는 돈이 없기 때문에 그것을 살 수 없다.
조건의 부사절을 이끄는 접속사	if (만약 ~라면)	If it is fine, we will go swimming. 만약 날씨가 좋다면, 우리는 수영하러 갈 것이다.
	unless = if ~ not (만약 ~하지 않으면)	You will get hurt unless you are careful. 네가 조심하지 않으면 다치게 될 거야.

TIP

시간이나 조건을 나타내는 부사절에는 현재 시제가 미래 시제를 대신한다.
After the movie is over, I'm going to eat something. 영화가 끝나면, 나는 뭔가를 먹으러 갈 것이다.

TIP

because of 뒤에는 문장이 아닌, 명사(구)가 온다.
She cannot go to the party because of her cold. 그녀는 감기 때문에 파티에 갈 수 없다.

3 상관접속사

두 개 이상의 단어가 서로 관련을 지어서 접속사의 역할을 하는 것을 상관접속사라고 한다.

상관접속사	예문
both A and B (A와 B 둘 다)	Both Elly and Mark went to the library. Elly와 Mark 둘 다 도서관에 갔다.
either A or B (A 아니면 B)	Either he or I am responsible for the accident. 그 아니면 내가 그 사고에 책임이 있다.
neither A nor B (A도 B도 아닌)	She knows neither Chris nor Jeff. 그녀는 Chris도, Jeff도 모른다.
not only A but also B = B as well A (A뿐만 아니라 B도)	Not only you but also James came from London. 너 뿐만 아니라 James도 런던에서 왔다. Joey likes hamburgers as well as pizza. Joey는 피자 뿐만 아니라 햄버거도 좋아한다.
not A but B (A가 아니라 B)	John is not a teacher but a carpenter. John은 선생님이 아니라 목수이다.

A   다음 괄호 안에서 알맞은 것을 고르시오.

1 I like dogs (but / so) hate cats.

2 (If / When) I arrived at home, I felt very tired.

3 It is not only useful (or / but) also important.

4 Both animals (and / but) plants need water.

5 Which is larger, this ball (or / so) that one?

6 I know the man (but / because) I have met him before.

7 He should choose either a desktop computer (or / nor) a notebook.

8 (While / Because) I was reading, my brother watched TV.

9 I will help my mom (before / after) I finish my homework.

10 When the exam (is / will be) over, we will go to the movies.

arrive 도착하다
useful 유용한
plant 식물
desktop 데스크탑
exam 시험

B   다음 빈칸에 알맞은 등위접속사를 쓰시오.

1 Would you like some tea _____ milk?

2 I turned on the radio, _____ it didn't work.

3 I ate toast _____ soup for breakfast.

4 It was Alice's birthday, _____ we decided to buy her present.

5 Emma _____ Heather aren't sisters.

6 Are you listening, _____ are you sleeping?

7 They didn't have breakfast, _____ they were very hungry.

8 She enjoys swimming, _____ her sister doesn't.

turn on 켜다
work 작동하다
decide 결정하다
present 선물

A 다음 문장에서 알맞은 접속사를 보기에서 골라 쓰시오. (단, 한 번씩만 쓸 것)

보기	both	because	either	if	while	until	when

director 감독
upset 속상한
wet 젖은
take a walk 산책하다

1 She is famous as _____ a director and actress.

2 Nick is always _____ upset or angry about something.

3 He was sleeping _____ I entered the classroom.

4 Her hair was wet _____ she didn't have an umbrella.

5 _____ I can't find your house, I'll give you a call.

6 I will wait here _____ you finish the work.

7 I did the dishes _____ my sister was talking a walk with her dog.

B 밑줄 친 부분을 바르게 고쳐 쓰시오.

rainbow 무지개
Spanish 스페인어
exercise 운동하다
regularly 규칙적으로

1 Both men <u>but</u> women like the actress. ➡ _____

2 <u>Until</u> you hurry up, you will be late. ➡ _____

3 <u>But</u> it stopped raining, I saw a rainbow. ➡ _____

4 Please wait for me <u>after</u> I make my choice. ➡ _____

5 He is not a human <u>and</u> a robot. ➡ _____

6 If you <u>will exercise</u> regularly, you will be heathy. ➡ _____

7 She can speak English <u>as and as</u> Spanish. ➡ _____

8 Billy is <u>either</u> tall nor short. ➡ _____

9 I stayed at home <u>because</u> weather. ➡ _____

C 다음 두 문장을 주어진 접속사를 이용하여 한 문장으로 바꿔 쓰시오.

run away 달아나다
sneakers 운동화
popular 인기 있는

1 He is not a singer. He is an actor. (not A but B)

   ➡ _____

2 He saw a policeman. He ran away. (when)

   ➡ _____

3 Birds are singing. It must be morning. (because)

   ➡ _____

4 She has white sneakers. She has black sneakers. (both A and B)

   ➡ _____

5 Enter your email address. Or enter your phone number. (either A or B)

   ➡ _____

6 This game is popular with children. It is popular with adults. (not only A but also)

   ➡ _____

D 우리말과 같은 뜻이 되도록 주어진 단어를 바르게 배열하시오.

plane 비행기
turn off 끄다
delicious 맛있는

1 너는 제주도에 갈 때 비행기를 탔니 아니면 배를 탔니? (plane, or, by, ship, by)

   ➡ Did you go to Jejudo _____ ?

2 나의 여동생은 그 개를 봤을 때, 울기 시작했다. (she, the dog, when, saw)

   ➡ My sister started to cry _____ .

3 아기가 자고 있기 때문에 너는 불을 꺼야 한다. (is, because, the, sleeping, baby)

   ➡ _____ , you should turn off the light.

4 그것은 맛있을 뿐만 아니라 건강에도 좋다.
   (also, only, but, not, good, for your health, delicious)

   ➡ It is _____ .

1 빈칸에 들어갈 알맞은 것을 고르시오.

> He got up _____ the alarm clock rang.

① when   ② so   ③ or
④ that   ⑤ although

2 빈칸에 들어갈 말이 순서대로 바르게 짝지어진 것을 고르시오.

> • I bought Alice a doll _____ it was her birthday.
> • Mom was angry, _____ I wrote her a letter.

① because of - but   ② because - so
③ because - but   ④ because - for
⑤ because of - so

3 빈칸에 공통으로 들어갈 말을 고르시오.

> • Let's go home _____ it rains.
> • Say sorry to her _____ it's too late.

① if   ② when   ③ but
④ before   ⑤ and

4 다음 우리말과 같은 뜻이 되도록 빈칸에 알맞은 것을 고르시오.

> 만약 내가 숙제를 끝내면, 너와 함께 야구를 보러 갈 것이다.
> = _____ I finish my homework, I'll go to a baseball game with you.

① Unless   ② Because   ③ While
④ When   ⑤ If

5 빈칸에 들어갈 말이 보기와 다른 것을 고르시오.

> _____ he didn't wear glasses, he could not watch the movie.

① I didn't go out _____ it rained.
② She didn't come _____ she was sick.
③ _____ I was tired, I went home early.
④ I got up late, _____ I had to hurry up.
⑤ The room was dark _____ there were no lights.

6 다음 우리말을 영어로 바르게 옮긴 것을 고르시오.

> 네가 발표 연습을 매일 한다면, 너는 떨지 않을 것이다.

① If you will practice your speech, you won't be nervous.
② If you practice your speech, you won't be nervous.
③ If you practice your speech, you are nervous.
④ If you practiced your speech, you are nervous.
⑤ If you will practice your speech, you won't nervous.

7 밑줄 친 부분의 쓰임이 나머지와 다른 것을 고르시오.

① If it is sunny tomorrow, I'll go to the zoo.
② If you have any questions, you can ask me.
③ I don't know if she will give me a present.
④ You will be late if you don't leave now.
⑤ If I have enough time, I will read a book.

practice 연습하다   nervous 긴장한   present 선물   enough 충분한

8 다음 중 접속사의 쓰임이 <u>어색한</u> 것을 고르시오.

① I took a shower after I came home.

② I cleaned my room because it was dirty.

③ Cathy studied at school until she was 16 years old.

④ Before I submitted the document, I checked it again.

⑤ He felt gloomy, so he showed a positive attitude.

9 밑줄 친 부분의 쓰임이 나머지와 <u>다른</u> 것을 고르시오.

① <u>When</u> did she fall asleep?

② <u>When</u> your meal is ready, I will call you.

③ <u>When</u> is your summer vacation?

④ Can you tell me <u>when</u> the next train will arrive?

⑤ <u>When</u> are you going to tell the truth?

10 밑줄 친 부분의 쓰임이 <u>잘못된</u> 것을 고르시오.

① This apple is sweet <u>and</u> sour.

② Not only you but <u>also</u> I like going camping.

③ She is from neither the U.S. <u>or</u> England.

④ Mary can go with me <u>either</u> on Friday or on Sunday.

⑤ Tom likes cooking, <u>so</u> he will learn more about it.

11 다음 중 어법상 <u>어색한</u> 문장을 고르시오.

① He is old but still strong.

② Is she Korean or Japanese?

③ My baby brother can't walk or speak.

④ She entered the restaurant and orders a meal.

⑤ My midterm exam is on Tuesday and Friday.

12 빈칸에 공통으로 들어갈 알맞은 말을 쓰시오.

- The soccer game was both exciting _____ interesting.
- Kate visited the site _____ reserved a ticket.

13 다음 두 문장이 같은 뜻이 되도록 빈칸에 들어갈 알맞은 말을 쓰시오.

If you don't get enough rest, you will feel tired.

= _____ _____ _____ enough rest, you will feel tired.

→ _____

14 다음 문장에서 어법상 <u>어색한</u> 부분을 찾아 바르게 고쳐 쓰시오.

I will go fishing with my father when he will finish fixing the computer.

_____ → _____

15 주어진 단어를 바르게 배열하여 다음 우리말을 영어로 쓰시오.

네가 음악을 크게 듣는다면, 너의 가족이 잠에서 깰 것이다.

(you, your family, wake up, listen to, if, music, loudly, will)

→ _____

_____

---

submit 제출하다 document 문서, 서류 gloomy 우울한 positive 긍정적인 attitude 태도 fall asleep 잠이 들다 order 주문하다
midterm exam 중간고사 reserve 예약하다

[1-2] 빈칸에 들어갈 알맞은 말을 고르시오.

1

> Please come to the party _____ seven o'clock.

① for   ② on   ③ in
④ by   ⑤ until

2

> I didn't play in the game _____ a headache.

① between   ② after   ③ during
④ because   ⑤ because of

3 빈칸에 공통으로 들어갈 말을 고르시오.

> • _____ dinner, she went to bed early.
> • _____ I had lunch, I drank a cup of coffee.

① Before   ② For   ③ After
④ Because   ⑤ If

4 빈칸에 들어갈 말이 순서대로 바르게 짝지어진 것을 고르시오.

> • There is a monkey _____ the tree.
> • It stopped snowing _____ the night.

① over - for   ② on - during
③ between - at   ④ on - for
⑤ over - during

5 밑줄 친 부분을 어법상 바르게 고친 것을 고르시오.

> If she <u>do</u> the laundry today, it will dry quickly.

① do   ② does   ③ will do
④ doing   ⑤ did

6 다음 두 문장을 접속사 before를 이용하여 한 문장으로 바꿔 쓰시오.

> We will go to the movies. We will reserve movie tickets online in advance.

➡ We will _____

_____

7 다음 두 문장을 한 문장으로 바꿔 쓸 때 빈칸에 들어갈 알맞은 말을 고르시오.

> • I had a cold.
> • I went to see a doctor.
> → I had a cold, _____ I went to see a doctor.

① because   ② so   ③ when
④ if   ⑤ until

8 다음 우리말을 영어로 바르게 옮긴 것을 고르시오.

> 만약 그가 아침을 먹지 않는다면, 집중력이 떨어질 것이다.

① If he has breakfast, he won't focus on others.
② After he has breakfast, he won't focus on others.
③ Because he has breakfast, he won't focus on others.
④ Unless he has breakfast, he won't focus on others.
⑤ When he has breakfast, he won't focus on others.

빈칸에 들어갈 말이 순서대로 바르게 짝지어진 것을 고르시오.

9

> She _____ ate _____ drank for a week.
>
> 그녀는 일주일 동안 먹지도 마시지도 않았다.

① not - but   ② both - and
③ either - or   ④ neither - nor
⑤ not only - but also

10

> A When will you leave for New York?
> B I'll leave _____ May 27.
> A How long will you stay there?
> B I will stay there _____ 3 weeks.

① in – during   ② in - in
③ on – for   ④ on - during
⑤ in - for

11 다음 중 어법상 틀린 것을 고르시오.

> I'll ① meet you ② in front of ③ your house ④ in 5:10 ⑤ on Sunday.

12 주어진 단어를 바르게 배열하여 다음 우리말을 영어로 쓰시오.

> 만약 그가 거짓말을 하면, 그의 코가 길어질 것이다.
>
> (his nose, tells a lie, grow, he, longer, if, will)

➡ _____
_____

13 다음 짝지어진 두 문장의 의미가 다른 것을 고르시오.

① I wrote in my diary after I fed the dog.
  = I fed the dog before I wrote in my diary.
② The bike is in front of the hospital.
  = The hospital is behind the bike.
③ Because it was cold, I wore a jacket.
  = It was cold, so I wore a jacket.
④ Not only Mia but also Tom are lawyers.
  = Tom as well as Mia are lawyers.
⑤ Both Sam and Pam had dinner.
  = Either Sam or Pam had dinner.

[14-15] Brian이 오늘 한 일을 메모한 것을 보고, 빈칸에 알맞은 말을 쓰시오.

Time	Things
1:00	- caught a cold - went to the hospital
7:00	- visited a restaurant - had dinner

14 이유를 나타내는 전치사구와 시간을 나타내는 전치사를 이용해 Brian이 오후 1시에 한 일을 쓰시오.

> Brian _____
> _____ 1:00.

15 등위접속사를 이용해 Brian이 저녁 7시에 한 일을 쓰시오.

> Brian _____
> _____

기초탄탄
GRAMMAR

Workbook

2

Happy House

기초탄탄
GRAMMAR
2
Workbook

Happy House

Contents

can, may

A 다음 두 문장이 같은 뜻이 되도록 빈칸에 알맞은 말을 쓰시오.

1 May I sit here?

➡ _____ I _____ here?

2 Can I use this computer?

➡ _____ _____ _____ this computer?

3 Can you speak English?

➡ _____ you _____ _____ _____ English?

4 Jina can't make spaghetti.

➡ Jina _____ _____ _____ _____ spaghetti.

B 주어진 단어와 우리말을 이용하여 빈칸에 알맞은 말을 쓰시오.

1 나는 지금 너무 바쁘다. 나는 너와 이야기할 수 없다. (talk)

➡ I'm too busy. I _____ _____ to you.

2 눈이 매우 많이 내린다. 그녀는 제 시간에 도착하지 않을지도 모른다. (arrive)

➡ It's snowing a lot. She _____ _____ _____ on time.

3 그는 아침에 일찍 일어나지 않을지도 모른다. (wake up)

➡ He _____ _____ _____ up early in the morning.

4 우리는 이제 그 엘리베이터를 이용할 수 있다. (use)

➡ We _____ _____ _____ _____ the elevator now.

5 나는 어제 시험 공부를 못했다. 나는 시험을 통과하지 못할지도 모른다. (pass)

➡ I didn't study for the exam yesterday. I _____ _____ _____ it.

---

a lot 많이, 매우 on time 제시간에 arrive 도착하다 wake up 잠에서 깨다 pass 통과하다, 합격하다

C 다음 문장을 괄호 안의 지시에 맞게 바꿔 쓰시오.

1 My brother can ride a bicycle. (부정문)

➡ _____

2 You can call me after 7 p.m. (의문문)

➡ _____

3 He is able to play the piano well. (의문문)

➡ _____

4 You may use it as a desk. (부정문)

➡ _____

5 My dad can cook pasta very well. (be able to 이용)

➡ _____

6 My back hurts. I cannot stand. (be able to 이용)

➡ _____

D 우리말과 같은 뜻이 되도록 주어진 단어를 이용하여 문장을 완성하시오.

1 나는 여동생을 위해 저녁을 만들 수 있다. (can, make dinner)

➡ _____

2 이 시계는 비쌀지도 모른다. (watch, may, expensive)

➡ _____

3 우리 반 학생들은 테니스 클럽에 가입해도 된다. (join, classmates, may)

➡ _____

4 우리는 함께 이 문제를 해결할 수 있다. (solve, are able to, together)

➡ _____

5 그들은 인터넷에서 무료 티켓을 얻을 수 있다. (get, can, a free ticket)

➡ _____

back 등, 허리 stand 서 있다 join 가입하다 expensive 비싼 solve 풀다, 해결하다 free 무료의

must, have to, should, had better

A 주어진 우리말을 이용하여 괄호 안에서 알맞은 것을 고르시오.

1 너는 좀 더 신중하게 생각해야 한다.
➡ You (must / had better) think more carefully.

2 그는 그 열쇠를 가져올 필요가 없다.
➡ He (must not / doesn't need to) take his key with him.

3 너는 컴퓨터 게임을 너무 많이 하면 안 된다.
➡ You (shouldn't / don't have to) play computer games too much.

B 빈칸에 must not 또는 don't have to를 넣어 문장을 완성하시오.

1 It was an accident. You _____ say sorry to me.

2 You _____ forget your homework. It's very important.

3 Don't hurry. We _____ leave yet.

4 She is always on time for her appointments. I _____ be late.

5 A sharp knife is dangerous. You _____ play with it.

6 We have sports day tomorrow. We _____ wear our school uniforms.

C 빈칸에 should 또는 shouldn't를 넣어 문장을 완성하시오.

1 It's an interesting movie. You _____ go to see it.

2 You have a test tomorrow. You _____ watch too much TV.

3 That sweater is too expensive. You _____ buy it.

4 Vietnamese food is very delicious. You _____ try it.

5 You and I are too young. We _____ drive a car.

6 John is sick in bed. He _____ go to school.

---

accident 사고, 우연 yet 아직 appointment 약속 sports day 운동회 날 sharp 날카로운 knife 칼 dangerous 위험한 school uniform 교복
Vietnamese 베트남의 sick in bed 앓아 누운

D 다음 문장을 괄호 안의 지시에 맞게 바꿔 쓰시오.

1 They have to take the subway in the morning. (과거형)

➡ _____

2 You have to study for the tests. (부정문)

➡ _____

3 I have to go home now. (의문문)

➡ _____

4 You had better wait for her here. (부정문)

➡ _____

5 She must buy a pair of shoes for the party. (have to 이용)

➡ _____

6 You should save money for the future. (had better 이용)

➡ _____

E 우리말과 같은 뜻이 되도록 주어진 단어를 이용하여 문장을 완성하시오.

1 당신은 여기에서 흡연을 해서는 안 된다. (must, smoke)

➡ _____

2 우리는 약한 사람들을 도와 주어야 한다. (should, weak people)

➡ _____

3 너는 울고 있는 아기를 떠나서는 안 된다. (must, leave, the crying baby)

➡ _____

4 그녀는 똑똑한 소녀임에 틀림 없다. (must, a smart girl)

➡ _____

5 우리는 사람을 외모로 판단하면 안 된다. (should, judge, by their appearance)

➡ _____

subway 지하철 wait 기다리다 a pair of shoes 구두 한 켤레 save 저축하다 weak 약한 leave 떠나다 crying 울고 있는 judge 판단하다
appearance 외모

There is/are

A 보기와 같이 다음 문장을 There is/are 구문으로 바꿔 쓰시오.

> 보기   A bottle is in the box.
> ➡ There is a bottle in the box.

1   A sandwich is on the plate.
➡ _____

2   Four seasons are in a year.
➡ _____

3   A rock is on the beach.
➡ _____

4   Footprints are in the sand.
➡ _____

B 주어진 우리말을 이용하여 빈칸에 알맞은 말을 쓰시오.

1   어젯밤에 약한 지진이 있었다.
➡ _____ _____ a weak earthquake last night.

2   공원에 쓰레기통이 없다.
➡ _____ _____ no trash cans in the park.

3   길 건너편에 버스정류장이 하나 있다.
➡ _____ _____ a bus stop across the street.

4   어제는 공원에 많은 사람들이 있었다.
➡ _____ _____ a lot of people in the park yesterday.

---

plate 접시   footprint 발자국   weak 약한   earthquake 지진   trash can 쓰레기통   February 2월

C 다음 문장을 괄호 안의 지시에 맞게 바꿔 쓰시오.

1 There is a parking lot behind the building. (부정문)
➡ _____

2 There is a large mirror on the wall. (의문문)
➡ _____

3 There are many old photos in the album. (의문문)
➡ _____

4 There is a church next to the school. (부정문)
➡ _____

5 There is a bridge over the river. (과거형)
➡ _____

6 There are many videos on the website. (과거형)
➡ _____

D 우리말과 같은 뜻이 되도록 주어진 단어를 이용하여 문장을 완성하시오.

1 9월에는 30일이 있다. (in September)
➡ _____

2 그 방에 의자가 하나 있다. (chair, in the room)
➡ _____

3 공기 중에는 많은 미세먼지가 있다. (fine dust, a lot of, in the air)
➡ _____

4 그릇 안에 약간의 밀가루가 있다. (in a bowl, some flour)
➡ _____

5 인터넷에는 유용한 정보가 아주 많이 있다. (useful information, on the Internet, very much)
➡ _____

parking lot 주차장   behind 뒤에   mirror 거울   next to ~ ~의 바로 옆에   bridge 다리   river 강   video 비디오   website 웹사이트
fine dust 미세먼지   flour 밀가루   useful 유용한

A 밑줄 친 it의 쓰임을 대명사와 비인칭 주어 중 알맞은 것을 골라 쓰시오.

1 We went to the museum yesterday. It was a lot of fun. _____

2 It is quite bright here. Come here. _____

3 I am going to go to the bank. It takes ten minutes on foot. _____

4 I have to finish my homework. I'll do it on my own. _____

5 Let's go outside! It's almost noon. _____

6 Be careful with the vase. It is very fragile. _____

B 밑줄 친 it에 유의하여 우리말로 해석하시오.

1 It is February 28 today.
   ➡ _____

2 It is going to rain this evening.
   ➡ _____

3 It is Friday today.
   ➡ _____

4 It is dark in the kitchen.
   ➡ _____

5 Give me the umbrella. I need it right now.
   ➡ _____

6 I drank a cup of juice. It was so cool.
   ➡ _____

7 It is time to get up. I'm so sleepy.
   ➡ _____

---

quite 상당히   on foot 걸어서   on one's own 혼자서   be careful 조심하다   fragile 깨지기 쉬운   dark 어두운   right now 당장   sleepy 졸린

C 괄호 안의 단어를 이용하여 다음 질문에 답하시오. (축약형으로)

1 What day is it today? (Thursday)

    ➡ _____

2 What date is it today? (October 12)

    ➡ _____

3 How is the weather? (cold and rainy)

    ➡ _____

4 What time is it now? (2:30)

    ➡ _____

5 What season is it? (spring)

    ➡ _____

6 How far is it from here to your house? (700 meters)

    ➡ _____

Chapter 2

D 우리말과 같은 뜻이 되도록 주어진 단어를 바르게 배열하시오.

1 런던에는 안개가 끼어 있다. (it, foggy, in London, is)

    ➡ _____

2 수요일 아침 8시였다. (and, it, Wednesday, in the morning, eight, was)

    ➡ _____

3 지금 하노이는 몇 시야? (is, time, it, in Hanoi, what)

    ➡ _____

4 오늘은 부모님의 결혼기념일이다. (my parent's, is, it, wedding anniversary)

    ➡ _____

5 겨울에는 바람이 많이 분다. (in winter, it, windy, very, is)

    ➡ _____

---

foggy 안개 낀   wedding anniversary 결혼기념일

형용사의 역할과 쓰임

A 다음 두 문장이 같은 뜻이 되도록 빈칸에 알맞은 말을 쓰시오.

1 This story is funny.

➡ This is a _____ _____.

2 This coat is thick.

➡ This is a _____ _____.

3 This honey is sticky.

➡ This is _____ _____.

4 This necklace is popular.

➡ This is a _____ _____.

5 Those drugs are effective.

➡ Those are _____ _____.

B 보기와 같이 다음 두 문장을 한 문장으로 바꿔 쓰시오.

> 보기   My mom knitted a muffler. The muffler is warm.
>
> ➡ My mom knitted a warm muffler.

1 I like the food. The food is spicy and salty.

➡ _____

2 She has a dress. The dress is white and beautiful.

➡ _____

3 My brother bought me a book. The book is helpful.

➡ _____

4 My teacher teaches me a subject. The subject is easy.

➡ _____

---

thick 두꺼운   honey 꿀   sticky 끈적거리는   necklace 목걸이   popular 인기 있는   drug 약   effective 효과적인   knit 뜨다, 짜다   muffler 목도리
mild 부드러운, 상냥한   helpful 도움이 되는   subject 과목

C 틀린 부분을 찾아 바르게 고쳐 문장을 다시 쓰시오.

1 The music made me sadly.

   ➡ _____

2 Her expression looks seriously.

   ➡ _____

3 He did wrong nothing yesterday.

   ➡ _____

4 We should not speak loudly in places public.

   ➡ _____

5 There is a full pencil case of pencils.

   ➡ _____

6 My family lives with pretty four puppies.

   ➡ _____

D 우리말과 같은 뜻이 되도록 주어진 단어를 바르게 배열하시오.

1 Stella는 그녀의 반에서 인기가 있다. (popular, Stella, in her class, is)

   ➡ _____

2 아침 운동은 나를 건강하게 만든다. (exercises, healthy, make, morning, me)

   ➡ _____

3 나는 신 음식을 먹는 것을 좋아한다. (foods, I, eating, sour, like)

   ➡ _____

4 그는 전 세계적으로 유명해졌다. (became, all, famous, around the world, he)

   ➡ _____

5 그녀의 목소리는 나에게 이상하게 들렸다. (voice, strange, sounded, her, to me)

   ➡ _____

sadly 슬프게도 expression 표정, 표현 seriously 심각하게 wrong 잘못된 loudly 시끄럽게 public 공공의 full of ~ ~로 가득찬 exercise 운동
voice 목소리 strange 이상한

A 빈칸에 many 또는 much를 넣어 문장을 완성하시오.

1 My sister has too _____ homework to do.

2 _____ people enjoyed watching the Olympics.

3 There are _____ seats in the baseball park.

4 James has very _____ interest in Korean history.

5 _____ dogs are running down the street.

6 How _____ sugar do you put in your coffee?

B 빈칸에 a few, few, a little, little 중 알맞은 것을 넣어 문장을 완성하시오.

1 Please give me _____ grape juice.

2 Mr. Kim will arrive in Seoul in _____ days.

3 This device uses _____ energy. It will save energy.

4 The actress is not famous at all. She has _____ fans.

5 Jeff picked up _____ coins on the street.

C 빈칸에 some 또는 any를 넣어 문장을 완성하시오.

1 Here are _____ interesting facts.

2 I don't have _____ money to go to the movie.

3 _____ animals use their tails to catch prey.

4 Can you think of _____ other ways?

5 He doesn't have _____ time for breakfast.

6 Do you do _____ special family activities?

baseball park 야구장 device 장치 save 아끼다 at all 전혀 pick up 줍다 coin 동전 fact 사실 prey 먹이 activity 활동

D 우리말과 같은 뜻이 되도록 주어진 단어를 바르게 배열하시오.

1 그들은 콘서트에서 많은 노래를 불렀다. (songs, a lot of, they, sang, at the concert)
➡ _____

2 너는 하루에 몇 개의 딸기를 먹니? (eat, how many, do, a day, strawberries, you)
➡ _____

3 몇몇의 학생들이 나를 보러 왔다. (students, me, came, a, see, few, to)
➡ _____

4 Jane은 책을 읽는 데 많은 시간을 보냈다. (reading, spent, too, time, Jane, much)
➡ _____

5 그녀는 회복될 희망이 거의 없다. (little, for her, to recover, is, there, hope)
➡ _____

6 그것은 은행으로부터 불과 몇 킬로미터 떨어져 있다. (is, only, kilometers, from, away, few, it, the bank, a)
➡ _____

7 그들은 발표를 준비할 약간의 시간이 있다. (a, prepare, time, they, presentation, their, have, little, to)
➡ _____

8 과도한 스트레스는 우리의 건강에 해롭다. (for, too, our health, stress, is, much, bad)
➡ _____

9 그는 산책과 캠핑과 같은 약간의 야외 활동을 한다.
(few, does, camping, like, outdoor activities, a, walking, he, and)
➡ _____

10 100세까지 사는 사람은 적다. (one hundred, to, few people, years old, be, live)
➡ _____

---

contest 대회   presentation 발표   be bad for ~ ~에 나쁘다   recover 회복되다   outdoor 야외의   hundred 백, 100

부사의 역할과 형태

A 다음 괄호 안에서 알맞은 것을 고르시오.

1 He was really (sad / sadly) about the exam results.

2 The young boy played the guitar very (good / well).

3 "Be quiet!" she said (angry / angrily).

4 She went to bed (late / lately) last night.

5 The dog barked (loud / loudly) in the morning.

6 We should eat our food (quiet / quietly).

7 Breath (deep / deeply) and you will be okay.

8 Alice put the books (neat / neatly) on the shelf.

9 He was (happy / happily) to meet her again.

10 I couldn't concentrate on my studies. I (hard / hardly) studied.

B 주어진 단어와 우리말을 이용하여 빈칸에 알맞은 말을 쓰시오. 단, 필요에 따라 단어를 변형시켜 쓰시오.

1 편안히 앉아서 눈을 감아주세요. (sit, comfortable)
  ➡ Please _____ _____ and close your eyes.

2 한국에서, 새 학기는 일반적으로 3월에 시작한다. (common, begin)
  ➡ In Korea, the new semester _____ _____ in March.

3 아침에 새들이 명랑하게 지저귀고 있었다. (sing, cheerful)
  ➡ The birds _____ _____ _____ in the morning.

4 그들은 그 상황을 면밀히 관찰해야 한다. (observe, close)
  ➡ They should _____ the situation _____.

---

bark 짖다 quietly 조용히 deep 깊은 deeply 깊게 neat 깔끔한 neatly 깔끔하게 breath 호흡하다 concentrate on ~ ~에 집중하다
hardly 거의 ~ 아니다 comfortable 편안한 cheerfully 명랑하게 observe 관찰하다 closely 면밀히

C 틀린 부분을 찾아 바르게 고쳐 문장을 다시 쓰시오.

1 She was a greatly poet and artist.

➡ _____

2 The sun shined bright in the sky.

➡ _____

3 I decided on the matter quick.

➡ _____

4 Don't worry. Everything will go good.

➡ _____

5 The window does not open easy.

➡ _____

D 우리말과 같은 뜻이 되도록 주어진 단어를 바르게 배열하시오.

1 그 기차는 곧 떠날 것이다. (leave, the train, shortly, will)

➡ _____

2 Helen은 친구가 오기를 끈기 있게 기다렸다. (her friend, Helen, patiently, to come, for, waited)

➡ _____

3 그 정치인은 그녀의 모든 질문에 정직하게 대답했다. (answered, of, honestly, the politician, all, her questions)

➡ _____

4 그 의사는 매우 조심스럽게 수술을 했다. (the operation, carefully, the doctor, very, performed)

➡ _____

poet 시인 artist 예술가 shine 빛나다 decide on ~ ~에 대해 결정하다 shortly 곧 patiently 끈기 있게 honestly 정직하게
politician 정치인 operation 수술 carefully 조심스럽게 perform 수행하다

A 빈칸에 들어갈 알맞은 말을 보기에서 골라 쓰시오.

> 보기   usually   sometimes   never   often   always

1 그는 종종 내가 역사 공부하는 것을 도와준다.
   ➡ He _____ helps me with history.

2 우리는 때때로 부모님을 위해 깜짝 파티를 계획한다.
   ➡ We _____ plan a surprise party for our parents.

3 나는 보통 소설책을 읽지만, 다른 때에는 잡지를 읽기도 한다.
   ➡ I _____ read novels, but I read magazines at other times.

4 그녀는 절대로 혼자서 공포 영화를 보지 않는다.
   ➡ She _____ goes to horror movies alone.

5 급행 열차는 항상 제 시간에 도착한다.
   ➡ The express train _____ arrives at the station on time.

B 다음 괄호 안에서 알맞은 것을 고르시오.

1 He (usually arrives / arrives usually) at school on time.

2 I remember her very well. I (never / often) saw her at the club.

3 I don't like musicals much. So I (always / seldom) see musicals.

4 I was disappointed with her. I will (always / never) apologize her.

5 How (sometimes / often) does your father go on business trips?

6 The player injured his arm. So he can (seldom / usually) play basketball.

help A with B A가 B하는 것을 돕다   express train 급행 열차   on time 제시간에   musical 뮤지컬   be disappointed with ~ ~에 실망하다
apologize 사과하다   business trip 출장   injure 부상을 입다

C 주어진 빈도부사를 알맞은 위치에 넣어 문장을 다시 쓰시오.

1 Lily tidies up her desk on weekends. (often)
➡ _____

2 He is late for work. (sometimes)
➡ _____

3 She rides the roller coaster at the amusement park. (never)
➡ _____

4 Acid rain hurts wild animals and plants. (usually)
➡ _____

5 Lisa cares about other people's feelings. (seldom)
➡ _____

6 Do you have lunch with him? (often)
➡ _____

Chapter 4

D 우리말과 같은 뜻이 되도록 주어진 단어를 바르게 배열하시오.

1 5 더하기 5는 항상 10이다. (ten, always, five, is, and, five)
➡ _____

2 그는 복권을 거의 구입하지 않는다. (seldom, a lottery ticket, he, purchases)
➡ _____

3 그는 식사 전에 손을 항상 씻는다. (before, his hands, eating, always, he, washes)
➡ _____

4 나는 햄버거와 같은 패스트푸드를 절대 먹지 않는다. (never, hamburgers, I, fast food, eat, like)
➡ _____

5 그녀는 종종 정치에 관한 책을 읽는다. (reads, politics, she, about, often, books)
➡ _____

---

tidy up 정리하다 roller coaster 롤러코스터 amusement park 놀이공원 acid rain 산성비 hurt 다치게 하다 wild 야생의 lottery ticket 복권
purchase 사다 like ~처럼 politics 정치

Who, What, Which

A 주어진 우리말을 이용하여 빈칸에 알맞은 의문사를 쓰시오.

1 네가 가장 좋아하는 영화는 무엇이니?

➡ _____ is your favorite movie?

2 누가 그 질문에 대답했니?

➡ _____ answered the question?

3 초록색과 파란색 중에 어떤 색을 더 좋아하니?

➡ _____ color do you like better, green or blue?

4 너는 어떤 종류의 스포츠를 할 수 있니?

➡ _____ kind of sport can you do?

5 커피와 차 중에 어떤 것을 원하세요?

➡ _____ do you want, coffee or tea?

B 밑줄 친 부분을 묻는 의문문을 완성하시오.

1 My father is a cook.

➡ _____ do?

2 Daniel reads the newspaper every day.

➡ _____ every day?

3 He ate a hamburger for lunch.

➡ _____ for lunch?

4 Emma studied English after school.

➡ _____ after school?

5 Tony and his brother are washing the window.

➡ _____ washing?

---

newspaper 신문 after school 방과 후에 wash 씻다, 닦다

C 다음 빈칸에 알맞은 의문사를 쓰시오.

1 A _____ time does she return?

   B She returns at noon.

2 A _____ lunchbox is this?

   B It's Tim's.

3 A _____ does your sister look like?

   B She is tall and blonde.

4 A _____ does he do after school?

   B He studies English

D 주어진 단어를 바르게 배열하여 대화를 완성하시오.

1 A _____ (date, today, is, what, the)

   B It's Saturday.

2 A _____ (him, the letter, to, wrote, who)

   B I wrote the letter to him.

3 A _____ (are, slippers, these, whose)

   B These are Mary's.

4 A _____ (do, prefer, or, the bus, which, you, the subway)

   B I prefer the subway.

5 A _____ (did, what, you, forget)

   B I forgot his address.

6 A _____ (the, knows, player, who)

   B Chris does.

---

return 돌아오다 at noon 정오에 look like ~ ~인 것처럼 보이다 blonde 금발인 forget 잊다 address 주소 player 선수

When, Where, Why, How

A   주어진 우리말을 이용하여 빈칸에 알맞은 의문사를 쓰시오.

1   너는 왜 그렇게 행복하니?

➡ _____ are you so happy?

2   너는 이 기계를 언제 사용하니?

➡ _____ do you use this machine?

3   어떻게 그것이 가능한가요?

➡ _____ is that possible?

4   내가 어디에서 너를 다시 만날 수 있니?

➡ _____ can I see you again?

B   다음 빈칸에 들어갈 알맞은 말을 쓰시오.

1   A _____ _____ is your brother?
    B He is 175cm tall.

2   A _____ _____ did you play basketball?
    B About three hours.

3   A _____ _____ do you go swimming?
    B Once a week.

4   A _____ _____ is this umbrella?
    B It's 5,000 won.

5   A _____ _____ calendars do you have?
    B I have three calendars.

6   A _____ _____ is it from here to the market?
    B It's three stops by subway.

---

machine 기계   use 사용하다   possible 가능한   calendar 달력   market 시장   stop 정류장

C 다음 빈칸에 알맞은 의문사를 쓰시오.

1　A _____ will he get back from New York?

　 B Next Friday.

2　A _____ can I buy the book?

　 B You can buy it at a bookstore.

3　A _____ are you always so busy?

　 B Because I have too much work.

4　A _____ do you study English conversation?

　 B I study it with native speakers.

D 주어진 단어를 바르게 배열하여 대화를 완성하시오.

1　A _____ (when, begin, the meeting, does)

　 B It begins at 3 'clock.

2　A _____ (he, be, a baker, does, want, why, to)

　 B Because he likes to make bread.

3　A _____ (your family, often, eat out, how, does)

　 B Once a month.

4　A _____ (the examination, where, take, you, did)

　 B At Woori Elementary School.

5　A _____ (spell, you, the word, how, do)

　 B D-I-F-F-E-R-E-N-T.

6　A _____ (does, the sale, when, end)

　 B On May 1.

---

get back from ~ ~에서 돌아오다 bookstore 서점 conversation 회화, 대화 native speaker 원어민 meeting 회의 baker 제빵사
eat out 외식하다 take an examination 시험을 보다 spell 철자를 말하다

비교급

A 다음 괄호 안에서 알맞은 것을 고르시오.

1 This subject is (easier / easyer) than that one.

2 His invention is as (useful / more useful) as her invention.

3 This shirt is (cheaper / more cheap) than that jacket.

4 The baseball park is (wider / more wide) than the basketball court.

5 My mom came back (earlier / more early) than my sister.

6 Brian's coat isn't as (thick / thicker) as my coat.

7 Jisu's English pronunciation is (good / better) than Mina's.

8 My dad eats (little / less) than usual for his health.

9 Alice's bag is (even / very) heavier than John's.

10 Tony's story is (surprisinger / more surprising) than Bill's.

B 빈칸에 들어갈 말을 보기에서 골라 적절한 형태로 바꿔 쓰시오. (단, 한 번씩만 쓸 것)

보기	active	much	well	dangerous	quiet	nice

1 My computer is _____ than yours.

2 A bike is _____ than a train.

3 This park is _____ than that restaurant.

4 James receives _____ pocket money than Jimmy.

5 Nick is _____ than Chris in P.E. class.

6 She can paint _____ than him.

---

subject 과목 invention 발명품 useful 유용한 baseball park 야구장 basketball court 농구장 wide 넓은 thick 두꺼운 pronunciation 발음
active 적극적인, 활동적인 receive 받다 pocket money 용돈 P.E. (physical education) 체육

C 밑줄 친 부분을 바르게 고쳐 문장을 다시 쓰시오.

1 Jenny's idea was more creative <u>as</u> David's.

　➡ _____

2 Ann is <u>generouser</u> with her time than Wendy.

　➡ _____

3 I can speak <u>so</u> loudly as my brother can.

　➡ _____

4 The KTX is <u>more quick</u> than the bus.

　➡ _____

5 The new process is <u>more simple</u> than the old one.

　➡ _____

6 Kate was <u>calmmer than</u> Susan in the situation.

　➡ _____

D 우리말과 같은 뜻이 되도록 주어진 단어를 이용하여 문장을 완성하시오.

1 그녀의 어머니는 그녀보다 현명하다. (wise)

　➡ _____

2 그 경찰관은 그 소년보다 용감했다. (brave, the policeman)

　➡ _____

3 너는 다음 번에 더 잘할 거야. (well, next time)

　➡ _____

4 나에게는 낚시가 캠핑보다 덜 지루하다. (fishing, camping, boring)

　➡ _____

5 채소는 패스트푸드보다 건강에 좋다. (vegetables, fast food, healthy)

　➡ _____

creative 창의적인　generous 너그러운　process 절차　quick 빠른　simple 간단한　calm 침착한　wise 지혜로운　brave 용감한　boring 지루한
vegetable 채소　healthy 건강한

A 다음 괄호 안에서 알맞은 것을 고르시오.

1 The eyes are the (more / most) important part of the body.

2 What are the (noisiest / most noisy) insects in the world?

3 No singer's voice is (as / more) beautiful as her voice.

4 The restaurant's service is the (baddest / worst) of all.

5 No sea (animal is / animals are) bigger than a whale.

6 The word is the longest (in / of) all the English words.

7 On the winter solstice, the daytime is the (shortest / shorttest) one of the year.

8 Christina is (the better / the best) singer in her country.

9 The woman teaches English the (good / best) at our school.

10 Olivia is the (fasionablest / most fashionable) student in her class.

B 빈칸에 들어갈 말을 보기에서 골라 적절한 형태로 바꿔 쓰시오. (단, 한 번씩만 쓸 것)

보기	early	accurate	exciting	safe	hard	essential

1 This is the _____ city in the world.

2 Jenny signed up for the yoga class the _____ of all.

3 This mattress is the _____ in the store.

4 The time of the clock is the _____ in my house.

5 It is the _____ event at the opening ceremony.

6 Sleep is the _____ element for all living animals.

insect 곤충   sea 바다   whale 고래   the winter solstice 동지 (the summer solstice 하지)   accurate 정확한   exciting 신나는   safe 안전한
essential 필수적인   sign up 등록하다, 가입하다   mattress 매트리스   opening ceremony 개막식   element 요소, 성분   living 살아 있는

C 밑줄 친 부분을 바르게 고쳐 문장을 다시 쓰시오.

1 This is the <u>strong</u> tree in our town.

   ➡ _____

2 My father is the <u>busy</u> person in my family.

   ➡ _____

3 This coffee is the <u>sweeter</u> of three.

   ➡ _____

4 The man can deliver the food the <u>faster</u> of all three men.

   ➡ _____

5 She overcame the <u>tougher</u> time in her life.

   ➡ _____

6 No other student is <u>more talkative</u> as Tom in our class.

   ➡ _____

D 우리말과 같은 뜻이 되도록 주어진 단어를 이용하여 문장을 완성하시오.

1 그 새는 세계에서 가장 작은 새이다. (tiny, in the world)

   ➡ _____

2 그 식당에서 어떤 음식도 파스타보다 맛있지 않다. (at the restaurant, delicious, the pasta)

   ➡ _____

3 이 컴퓨터는 품질에 있어서 최고이다. (good, in quality)

   ➡ _____

4 이곳은 이 지역에서 가장 고급스러운 호텔이다. (luxurious, in this area)

   ➡ _____

5 Bobby의 책상은 셋 중에서 가장 더럽다. (dirty)

   ➡ _____

strong 튼튼한   deliver 배달하다   overcame 극복하다   tough 힘든, 어려운   talkative 수다스러운   tiny 아주 작은   quality 질, 우수함
luxurious 호화로운   area 지역, 구역

A   어법상 틀린 부분을 찾아 바르게 고쳐 쓰시오.

1   No park here, please.   _____ ➡ _____

2   Be listen to your teacher.   _____ ➡ _____

3   Mixes it with water.   _____ ➡ _____

4   Don't nervous. You can do it.   _____ ➡ _____

5   Let's open not the door.   _____ ➡ _____

B   다음 문장을 긍정명령문과 부정명령문으로 바꿔 쓰시오.

1   You take this pill every evening.
     ➡ _____
     ➡ _____

2   You clean up your desk.
     ➡ _____
     ➡ _____

3   You memorize English words.
     ➡ _____
     ➡ _____

4   You write in your diary every day.
     ➡ _____
     ➡ _____

5   You make a weekly plan.
     ➡ _____
     ➡ _____

park 주차하다   mix 섞다   nervous 긴장한   pill 알약   clean up 청소하다   memorize 암기하다, 기억하다   weekly 매주의, 주간의   plan 계획

C 다음 문장을 명령문으로 바꿔 쓰시오.

1 You must not spill milk.

→ _____

2 You must not eat fast food too often.

→ _____

3 You must not swim in the river.

→ _____

4 You must not press that button.

→ _____

5 You must not forget the papers.

→ _____

D 우리말과 같은 뜻이 되도록 주어진 단어를 이용하여 문장을 완성하시오.

1 잠시만 기다려 주세요. (wait, a bit)

→ _____

2 은행까지 가는 길을 알려주세요. (tell, way to)

→ _____

3 화분을 햇빛이 잘 드는 곳에 놓아라. (place, plant, in a sunny area)

→ _____

4 그녀의 사과를 받아들여라. (accept, apology)

→ _____

5 영화관에서 큰 소리로 말하지 마라. (talk, in a loud voice, in the theater)

→ _____

6 다른 사람의 사생활을 존중해라. (respect, others' privacy)

→ _____

spill 쏟다, 흘리다 press 누른다 button 버튼, 단추 forget 잊어버리다 wait 기다리다 place 놓다, 두다 accept 받아들이다 respect 존중하다
privacy 사생활

Chapter 7

A 다음 문장에서 밑줄 친 부분을 바르게 고쳐 쓰시오.

1 <u>What</u> happy the girl is! ➡ _____

2 <u>What</u> soft the silk cloth is! ➡ _____

3 <u>How</u> hot tea it is! ➡ _____

4 <u>How</u> a beautiful voice she has! ➡ _____

5 <u>How</u> a long hall this is! ➡ _____

6 <u>What</u> foolish he is! ➡ _____

7 How cute those puppies <u>is</u>! ➡ _____

8 What a <u>highly</u> mountain it is! ➡ _____

B 다음 문장을 감탄문으로 바꿔 쓸 때, 빈칸에 알맞은 말을 쓰시오.

1 It was a very difficult test.
➡ _____ it was!

2 The sunlight is really warm.
➡ _____ the sunlight is!

3 His Chinese is really perfect.
➡ _____ his Chinese is!

4 The teacher is very friendly.
➡ _____ the teacher is!

5 The nurse is a very brave person.
➡ _____ the nurse is!

6 He brought a really heavy bag.
➡ _____ he brought!

soft 부드러운 silk 실크, 비단 cloth 옷감 hall 복도, 현관 foolish 어리석은 mountain 산 difficult 어려운 sunlight 햇빛 friendly 친절한
nurse 간호사 heavy 무거운

C 주어진 말을 이용하여 다음 문장을 감탄문으로 바꿔 쓰시오.

1   She speaks really slowly. (how)

➡ _____

2   The cookies are very hard. (how)

➡ _____

3   She made a very funny face. (what)

➡ _____

4   He has a very powerful voice. (what)

➡ _____

5   The strawberries are really sweet. (how)

➡ _____

6   Basketball is a very exciting sport. (what)

➡ _____

D 우리말과 같은 뜻이 되도록 주어진 단어를 바르게 배열하시오.

1   그는 정말 독특한 별명을 가졌구나! (nickname, has, a, he, unique, what)

➡ _____

2   그 배우들은 정말 연기를 잘하는구나! (the actors, well, how, act)

➡ _____

3   그 나비는 정말 아름다운 날개를 가졌구나! (wings, beautiful, has, the butterfly, what)

➡ _____

4   너의 아버지는 정말 건강에 좋은 음식을 드시는구나! (father, eats, what, food, your, healthy)

➡ _____

powerful 강력한   strawberry 딸기   unique 독특한   wing 날개

A 빈칸에 들어갈 알맞은 말을 보기에서 골라 쓰시오. (단, 한 번씩만 쓸 것)

| 보기 | in | before | at | on |

1 우리 정오에 만나자.
➡ Let's meet _____ noon.

2 그는 항상 저녁에 산책한다.
➡ He always takes a walk _____ the evening.

3 Cathy의 생일 파티는 8월 3일이다.
➡ Cathy's birthday party is _____ August 3.

4 나는 시험 전에 책을 한 번 더 본다.
➡ I read my books again _____ an exam.

B 빈칸에 들어갈 알맞은 말을 보기에서 골라 쓰시오. (단, 한 번씩만 쓸 것)

| 보기 | on | in front of | at | in |

1 Alice는 그 회의에 나타나지 않았다.
➡ Alice didn't show up _____ the meeting.

2 그 아이는 벤치 위에 누워 있다.
➡ The kid is lying _____ the bench.

3 그것은 한국에서 가장 인기 있는 스포츠이다.
➡ It is the most popular sport _____ Korea.

4 많은 사람들 앞에서 말하는 것은 긴장된다.
➡ Speaking _____ many people makes me feel nervous.

---

noon 정오   take a walk 산책하다   show up 나타나다   lie 누워 있다   popular 인기 있는

C 틀린 부분을 찾아 바르게 고쳐 문장을 다시 쓰시오.

1 Don't sit with the chair. It is wet.

➡ _____

2 Most flowers bloom at spring.

➡ _____

3 The new school year starts on March.

➡ _____

4 Victoria will arrive here until 10 o'clock.

➡ _____

5 What do you do at April Fools' Day?

➡ _____

6 She cut the watermelon by a knife.

➡ _____

D 우리말과 같은 뜻이 되도록 주어진 단어를 바르게 배열하시오.

1 그녀의 인형들은 탁자 위에 있는 상자 안에 있다. (in, are, dolls, the table, on, her, the box)

➡ _____

2 Amy는 어린이날에 가족과 함께 즐거운 시간을 보냈다.
(had, family, Children's Day, Amy, a great time, on, with, her)

➡ _____

3 그 버스는 두 개의 공항 사이를 운행한다. (between, the bus, airports, two, runs)

➡ _____

4 은행 앞에서 잠시만 기다려주세요. (the bank, wait, please, for a minute, in front of)

➡ _____

5 책상과 피아노 사이에 탁자가 하나 있다. (is, the piano, a table, there, the desk, between, and)

➡ _____

bloom 꽃이 피다 arrive 도착하다 April Fools' Day 만우절 watermelon 수박 doll 인형 for a minute 잠시 동안
between A and B A와 B사이에

A 빈칸에 들어갈 알맞은 말을 보기에서 골라 쓰시오. (단, 한 번씩만 쓸 것)

| 보기 | so | but | or | and |

1 나의 이름은 Paul이고 New York 출신이다.
➡ My name is Paul, _____ I'm from New York.

2 그는 이번 목요일에 시험이 있어서 열심히 공부하고 있다.
➡ He has an exam this Thursday, _____ he is studying hard.

3 이 과일은 신선하지만 안 좋은 냄새가 난다.
➡ This fruit is fresh, _____ it smells bad.

4 넌 초밥 또는 피자 중에 어느 것을 좋아하니?
➡ Which do you like, sushi _____ pizza?

B 보기에서 알맞은 것을 골라 문장을 완성하시오. (단, 한 번씩만 쓸 것)

보기	it is raining outside	your brother
	the bus left	I was twelve years old
	you walk more quickly	I didn't have enough water

1 After _____, Emma arrived.

2 You will miss the subway unless _____.

3 I was thirsty, but _____.

4 We can't go out because _____.

5 Not only you but also _____ knows me.

6 When _____, I lived in Toronto.

smell 냄새가 나다 sushi 초밥 enough 충분한 miss 놓치다 subway 지하철

C   다음 두 문장을 괄호 안의 접속사를 이용하여 한 문장으로 바꿔 쓰시오.

1   He is poor. He cannot buy the car. (because)

➡ _____

2   You study hard. You can speak English well. (if)

➡ _____

3   She was a child. She wanted to be a doctor. (when)

➡ _____

4   Christina called you. You were away. (while)

➡ _____

5   She was tired. She studied hard for the test. (but)

➡ _____

6   Say sorry to him. It's too late. (before)

➡ _____

D   우리말과 같은 뜻이 되도록 주어진 단어를 바르게 배열하시오.

1   자러 가기 전에 이를 닦아라. (you, teeth, before, brush, go to bed, your)

➡ _____

2   네가 돌아올 때까지 나는 여기 있을게. (here, be, come back, you, I'll, until)

➡ _____

3   그는 버스를 놓쳤기 때문에 학교에 늦었다. (late for, missed, he, because, the bus, school, was, he)

➡ _____

4   코트를 입지 않는다면, 너는 감기에 걸릴 것이다. (unless, catch a cold, you, will, a coat, wear, you)

➡ _____

5   Noah와 Lua는 둘 다 수학을 잘한다. (math, Lua, and, are good at, both, Noah)

➡ _____

be away 부재중이다, 떨어져 있다   be good at ~ ~를 잘하다